New Beginnings

Co-Parenting Course Workbook

Co-Parenting Divorce Workbook

Kristine Turner, Ph.D.

MW00947182

A New Beginnings™ Publication
All Rights Reserved
Copyright 2014 by Kristine Turner

No part of this book may be reproduced or transmitted in any form or by any means, electronic or mechanical, including photocopy, recording or by any information storage and retrieval system, without permission, in writing from the publisher.

KRISTINE TURNER, PH.D.
558 CASTLE PINES PARKWAY
UNIT B-4 #364
CASTLE ROCK, CO 80108
TEL: 303.706.9424
FAX: 303.814.0365

Kristine.Turner@NewBeginningsCoParenting.com

DivorceAdviceForChildren.com
NewBeginningsCoParenting.com

ISBN: 1532782802

Table of Contents:

Section 1:

New Beginnings Co-Parenting Course Workbook

p. 4

Section 2:

Mommy and Daddy are Getting a Divorce

p. 37

Section 3:

Guide to a Smart Divorce

p. 55

Section 4:

Divorce Flow Charts

p. 102

CHAPTER 1
FACTS ABOUT DIVORCE

❖   Divorce is NORMAL!

❖   One of two marriages ends in divorce.

❖ 60% of divorces occur for people between the ages of 25-39.

❖ Over 1,000,000 children are affected by divorce each year.

❖ Half of all children of divorce will grow up in families where the parents stay angry at one another.

❖ Three out of every five children of divorce will feel rejected by a parent.

❖ 70% of all children born in 1980 will spend time in a single parent family.

❖ For divorcing partners, 75% of women and 80% of men remarry within five years.

❖ More second marriages end in divorce compared to first marriages.

❖ Currently, more people are part of second marriages than of a first marriage. The di vorce rate is also higher for second marriages vs. first marriages.

❖ One of five children lives in a single parent home.

❖ Younger girls may adjust better, both socially and academically, than boys.

❖ Girls may have a more difficult time in adjusting to remarriages than boys.

❖ Children of divorce have a higher rate of divorce than the children whose parents have stayed married. This is largely due to the fact that children of divorce have a model before them that suggests divorce as a viable or acceptable solution to marital problems.

❖ 25% of children of divorce drop out of high school.

❖ Children will be full of guilt and will need to know that the divorce is not their fault.

     40% require psychological counseling.

     65% have poor relationships with their fathers.

     30% have poor relationships with their mothers.

❖ Children will have a great deal of anger because of the events occurring that are be yond their control.

❖ Unless there has been abuse or neglect, most children wish their parents would re concile and sometimes will try to get their parents back together.

❖ It is common for children to idealize the missing parent.

❖ Children will go through a grieving process than can last 2 to 5 years.

POST-DIVORCE PARENTING RECOMMENDATIONS

- ❖ Set limits and discipline your children. They need to experience order at a time that seems like chaos, to them.
- ❖ Let the children keep in touch with relatives of both parents.
- ❖ Younger children may need repeated explanations about what is happening.
- ❖ Children may express the stress they are feeling as absent-mindedness, nervousness, weariness, moodiness, etc.
- ❖ Give your children insight and empathy, not pity.
- ❖ Keep changes to a minimum so your children can adjust to the new circumstances.
- ❖ Do not burden your children with financial worries.
- ❖ Children will have to deal with feelings of shame and rejection. Create an atmosphere that allows children to love both parents.
- ❖ Step-families can create an uncomfortable situation for children. The biological parent should remain the disciplinarian for a while.
- ❖ After a divorce or separation, parents will face a host of challenges that make parenting difficult. Take care of yourself and keep trying.
- ❖ There are many ways to divorce and to parent after divorce, however, some methods and parenting choices are superior to others.
- ❖ If divorce is the right solution to the problem it may decrease the conflict over time. It is possible to have had a bad marriage and still have a good divorce.

Anything is possible once you learn how it can be done.

CHAPTER 2

USEFUL TIPS FOR HELPING YOUR CHILDREN MORE EFFECTIVELY DEAL WITH DIVORCE

1. Listen to your children. Spend time sitting quietly with your children, allowing them to talk about their day and their feelings. Make eye contact with them.
2. Reassure your children that you will be available to them.
3. Show your children, through your actions, that you are trustworthy.
4. Reassure your children that they will continue to have a relationship with both parents.
5. Continue to set limits and discipline your children, as structure is helpful to them.
6. Encourage children to express their feelings, (including sadness, loss, hurt, anger, guilt, helplessness, or fear) even if what they say is hard to hear.
7. Encourage children to express their opinions.
8. Demonstrate your love on a daily basis.
9. Explain changes in concrete terms. Show them where each parent will live, reassure them that there will be enough food, and money. Don't bother them with the details, refrain from sharing concerns about finances or residences with them.
10. Try to use a business-like communication model with the other parent in order to discuss the needs of your children.
11. Develop a workable parenting plan.
12. Help children adapt to both of their homes, e.g. toothbrush, clothes, toys, books, at both homes.
13. Keep both parents involved.
14. Keep children out of the middle.

Tips For Children Coping With Divorce

1. Understand that it is not your fault. Your parent's arguments and divorce are not your fault and are not under your control.

2. You don't need to solve your parents problems. Parents shouldn't ask you to take sides, relay messages or keep secrets. If they do, tell them that you would prefer to stay out of the situation.

3. Leave the room when your parents argue.

4. Understand that going through a divorce is hard on everyone. Many families have parents who divorce, and the confusing, sad, or scary feelings you may be experiencing are normal and will eventually go away.

5. Try to express your feelings. Talk to someone you can trust.

6. Ask your parents for the things you may need, such as time together; to be kept out of the middle of the divorce; to be trusted if you don't want to talk at the moment; to be allowed to love the other parent; to be allowed to express all kinds of feelings, even if it may hurt your parents.

7. Remember, every person gets angry at times, and you are not terrible for having angry thoughts and feelings even toward your parents.

8. Having angry "thoughts" toward someone will not cause that person harm.

9. Remember, the best thing you can do for yourself is act your age. Don't go back to being a baby, and don't try to be too grown-up.

10. If your parents try to win you over to their side of the story; tell them you want to be free to love both of your parents.

11. Don't take sides against one of your parents. It will make it much harder to develop a bond with the parent you alienated.

12. Keep in mind that although your parents are no longer husband and wife, they will always be your mom and dad.

How to Make Your Child Feel SPECIAL Every Day
by Vicki Lansky (Author)

❖ List your child's special qualities on a piece of paper and hang it - maybe even frame it.

❖ Read your child's baby book with him/her and tell stories about baby and toddler days.

❖ If your child routinely arrives home before you do, leave a "Welcome Home" note or a message to be played on a tape recorder.

❖ Leave an "I Love You" note in their backpack or lunch box.

❖ Send your child cards in the mail. Kids of all ages love receiving mail.

❖ Display your children's artwork and photos.

❖ Do show up at your child's practices, games, performances and recitals.

❖ Give your child a hug everyday.

❖ With younger children, play "hide and seek", thumb wrestle and push them in a swing as long as they like.

❖ A "nightly rake" - five minutes of back scratching, once in bed, is always a special treat.

❖ Take your child to your office so they can picture where you are and what you do all day.

❖ Play a board game or card game of their choice.

❖ Let your child hear you praise him or her to others. Kids love to hear good things about themselves, especially when they "accidentally overhear you."

❖ Listen; really listen, when your child talks to you. There is nothing more significant than being paid attention to (and, therefore, being valued) to make one feel special.

❖ Catch your child "in the act of being good." This will increase the likelihood of desired behavior happening again by focusing on the positive, not the negative acts.

Divorce doesn't end the family, it merely changes the structure.

PREDICTORS OF A
GOOD DIVORCE

Your ability to meet these criteria will largely determine how the divorce plays out for you and your family.

- ❖ Never bad-mouth the other parent in front of children. Parents who bad-mouth each other are in essence bad-mouthing their children because children identify with their parents and see themselves as like mom in some ways and like dad in other ways. Therefore, when you bad-mouth a parent your child hears the message as though you are bad-mouthing them.
- ❖ Quick resolution of conflict - no fighting in front of children
- ❖ Your ability to put yourself in your children's shoes
- ❖ Your ability to really listen to your children
- ❖ A smooth transition as things change - The more fluid, and the least amount of conflict the better.
- ❖ Keep your family a "family" - The message you send your children about what constitutes a family matters. Your children still have a mother and a father. Only the structure of the family has changed, however your family is still a family. This is an important message to impart to your child/children.

Research suggests that the TWO most damaging things that can occur during a divorce are:

1) Parental conflict
2) Parental loss

Make sure you do everything you can, take the "high road", to ensure that your children do not continue to witness any parental conflict and/or suffer the loss of a parent because of divorce.

Children should be allowed access to both parents following a divorce. Children who rarely see mom or dad after a divorce wonder "why" their parent would abandon them. They often come to see themselves as unlovable. Children who witness continued conflict between their parents do very poorly in a divorce and can never truly adjust to the impact of the divorce.

It is important that children continue to have lasting relationships with both parents after the divorce, as they define themselves, and come to understand themselves, based upon who their parents are.

Although you, as a parent, will experience the loss of your marital partner, your child should not have to grieve the same loss, as he or she should be able to retain a relationship with both parents.

CHAPTER 4

POSITIVE PARENTING

❖ Both parents need to tell children about the divorce, re-telling the story is okay. Repeat this message from time to time with your children.

That the:
> Divorce Is Final
> It was an Adult Decision
> It was not their fault

❖ It is important that children realize that they are not responsible for your divorce and that they cannot put you back together.

❖ Don't say 'Mommy and Daddy fell out of love' ...kids will worry that you can fall out of love with them. It is, therefore, extremely important to reiterate to children that parents will always love them and that divorce does not mean that the children lose a parent.

❖ In order to avoid parental loss, it is important to re-assure your child/children that you are available: (i.e. in person, by pager, via phone, e-mail, letters, etc.)

❖ Parents don't need to change their entire routine, however, they need to send the message to their children that they (the kids) matter and are important.

❖ Children do not need to be adversely affected by divorce.

❖ There are things you can do to protect children from the negative affects of divorce.

1. Reassure them you are available and there for them. Children often wonder, "can parents divorce me too?"

2. Make sure one or both parents provide essential nurturing (i.e., hugs and kisses.)

3. Children need someone who holds expectations for them. Be careful not to "parentify" - remain consistent with what your expectations were before the divorce.

4. Provide an area or situation in which their voice is heard. This lets them know they matter. "Kids need their say, not necessarily their way."

5. Actively listen. Most parents only spend 1½ minutes per day actively listening to their children. Try to increase this by becoming an active listener. Allow children to express their feelings. Do not be afraid to ask about their negative feelings. Let them know that all their feelings are O.K.

The average parent spends most of their time in directional or command based conversation with their children, i.e. "eat your breakfast", "do your homework", "please help your sister with her chores", etc. Parents do not do much back and forth interactive listening with their children.

Your children will have a reaction to your divorce and it is important to make sure that they can talk about their feelings and concerns with their parents.

6. Provide routine, consistency and dependability. Re-establish family rituals such as a special "Pizza Night", or watching your favorite TV shows together or reading aloud from their favorite book before bed. Remember that routine gives kids a sense of control and power in a healthy way.

7. See to it that they get support away from home - therapy, sports, grandparents and church. Encourage involved grandparents to come to a parenting after divorce seminar and/or read the material here on the subject.

We divorce in hopes that things will get better, in life we get what we look for ...

CHAPTER 5

DOS AND DON'TS

- ❖ NEVER try to get support from your children. They may pull for you to depend on them out of their fear of abandonment. In the end, they will only get confused.
- ❖ Adults benefit from getting support; however it should not come from their children.
- ❖ Children should be able to come to their parents for support, not the other way around.
- ❖ Do depend on other adults for support. Parents should instead seek outside support from other adults, co-workers, friends, adult family members, therapists, clergy, etc.
- ❖ Don't parentify kids. Do not make them your friend. They need to be your children and you need to be their parent. It is okay to have children increase their level of responsibility a little bit post-separation, however, they should not suddenly become a "mini-parent" in the household. Their chore load should remain similar to their peer group's.

Don't tell children too many specifics about the divorce.

You should acknowledge the divorce itself, and that it is occuring, and kids can learn about the emotional impact of divorce - including your anger or sadness, but it will not benefit them to know the adult details (who had the affair, who couldn't mange the finances, who was the ice queen, etc.)

A common way to address your anger is to state that you don't see things the same way as the other parent, but make sure that your children feel that they don't have to take sides in the matter.

- ❖ Do remain a good parent/role model. Children will emulate their parents during the divorce process. They will react behaviorally as they see their parents reacting.

Interestingly, children tend to emulate dad's style of anger management more often than mom's style.

❖ Do develop your own "new identity". Allow yourself time (1- 3 years) to heal and rebuild your life. Ask yourself tough questions; learn about yourself before you start dating again. (i.e., "Why was I attracted to my former spouse?", "What worked in the marriage? Why?" "What didn't? Why?" "What type of person am I better suited to be around?" "What types of people are better for me to associate with? Why?"

❖ Don't criticize your former spouse in front of the children. Children tend to identify with and understand themselves based upon who their parents are. Therefore bad-mouthing the other parent when around the child/children often hurts the child more than the other parent?

❖ You need to be dependable. Say what you mean and mean what you say. In short, do what you say you are going to do.

❖ Do create a workable parenting time agreement and re-evaluate it yearly.

Although divorce is the ending of one chapter in life, it is also the beginning of another.

CHAPTER 6

THE FIVE STAGES OF GRIEF

DENIAL AND ISOLATION is the initial period of not accepting the reality of the death, divorce, or other loss. It is a natural defense that allows one enough time to accept what is happening. You may feel numb or in shock. You may say for instance, "This can't be happening to me or my family." Children may find themselves saying, "My mom's not gone, she's on a business trip."

ANGER is an intense feeling of rage, envy or resentment, and may be targeted at innocent by-standers, (i.e., your children). Often one feels anger over being let down and may act out feelings in a variety of inappropriate ways. Finding an acceptable way to express anger is an integral part of the healing process. Remember, anger is normal in divorce situations.

BARGAINING is a period of wanting to fix things that are beyond our control. We might say things like, "If only I had done such and such..." Often we feel guilt for what has happened and may blame ourselves. Children may think the divorce is their fault and may be extra good thinking that then you will get back together.

DEPRESSION occurs when the reality of the loss sets in. At this stage you may feel despair. You may question your ability to deal with your sadness and may turn to unhealthy coping devices to ease your pain. Overeating, sleep disorders, excessive alcohol consumption, and drugs are all manifestations of a depressed state.

During this stage, you need nurturing and support and need healthy ways to live with your sadness and to overcome any unrealistic guilt you may feel.

ACCEPTANCE is the final stage of grief. It is a time when change is no longer a threat. Depending upon the circumstances, you might be more optimistic about the future or more accepting of your present circumstances.

KEY POINTS TO REMEMBER:

❖ It is not uncommon for parents to be in separate stages. Children always follow their parents through these stages; therefore, children cannot get to acceptance unless one of their parents does.

❖ Going through these stages is a necessary process towards healing that may or may not go in this exact order.

CHAPTER 7

CHILD DEVELOPMENT

Infants

Normal development -Infants are learning whether they can trust the "world" to meet their needs. They are bonding, but do not realize that objects/people exist when they are out of their view. They require parents to meet all their needs. Infants are often fearful of new things: stranger and separation anxiety are classic examples of this behavior.

Infants need consistency, predictability, and a gradual introduction to new environments. They tend to react negatively to chaotic situations. They may experience divorce as a general sense of abandonment.

Toddlers 1-3 Years

Normal development -Toddlers are learning about autonomy ("mine") and power/control.

They are dealing with the desire to be both independent and dependent. They are testing their competence on many levels as they acquire basic skills. They are working on language skills and motor skills. They are also learning the difference between the sexes, and find both parents important for sex role development, (e.g. the same sex parent for their own understanding of themselves and the other sex parent for differentiation and autonomy.) They are unable to comprehend time, and often engage in magical thinking/fantasy play.

Toddlers need reassurance that they are not responsible for the divorce, as they are egocentric in their thinking. They need continuity, basic love, food, shelter, etc. They need predictable routines everyday, and need to rehearse how things will work in order to feel comfortable with changes.

Children 3 - 5 Years

Normal development - Young children of this age group are learning about their own abilities and taking initiative. They actively explore and desire to learn. They are learning to separate themselves from others, and are learning to see themselves as separate from their parents. They now understand the power of words; however, their thinking is very concrete. Children in this age group need praise for their efforts and encouragement in their efforts to plan and venture forward. Mistakes should be reviewed from the aspect of what the child has learned, as opposed to being treated as failures. Children of this age should never be put down for their failings, or their feelings.

Children 6 -12 Years

School age children are learning to be industrious in their activities. They are developing their social skills, and are applying their abilities to technical and social situations. They are into moralistic behavior and understanding right from wrong. Although many may still show feelings, they often need help expressing them. If not given a chance to express feelings, these children will act them out in their behavior.

School age children need to take control and responsibility for their decisions and actions. They are becoming somewhat less egocentric and start to develop empathy for others. They are often into super heroes, and strive to be successful, and popular. They are also able to grasp the concept of binary thinking (that others can have different, but equally valid ideas).

School age children need to have their feelings recognized, but not rescued. They need to be heard. They need to know that their parents understand their fears and opinions; however, they are also able to understand that their parents may have different opinions. Children need to be allowed to express their anger over their parents divorce. Children of this age often try to take on the role of the opposite parent with whom they are residing; this "parentification" of the child is detrimental to their development.

Teenagers 12 -18 Years

Teenagers are establishing a sense of personal identity. They are more in touch with themselves and their own personality and preferences. They are separating from the family, and transferring alliances from family to peer groups. Parents continue to set outer boundaries and limits; however, peer groups now offer a supportive audience for experimentation.

Teenagers often rebel against the establishment, but also fear independence and the loss of their childhood. They may act invincible.

Teenagers need parental support as much as any other age group, and sometimes more, although they may be hesitant to ask for support. Teenagers need to be allowed to express their feelings and opinions in their own time and in their own way. They need to be trusted, and parents should assume competence until incompetence is exhibited.

Parents are often seen as an embarrassment - a 'dinosaur'. Because teenagers are close to adulthood, it is easy for them to assume a parental role. This "parentification" of teenagers is unhealthy and should be discouraged.

Parents need to differentiate between the teenager's need to see the parent versus the parents need to see their child. There is often a push and pull dynamic in operation.

Although you cannot control your teenager's thinking and desires, you can be clear about your expectations.

POSSIBLE BEHAVIOR OR REACTIONS OF CHILDREN - BY AGE

All children have reactions to a divorce. The most common are regression, clinginess, fearfulness, and emotional instability.

On-going parental conflict is the factor most likely to cause poor adjustment in children of all ages. If parents can keep their conflict to a minimum, especially in front of the children, then the negative affects of divorce are more likely to be brief rather than long lasting.

If your child is reluctant to spend time with you or your former spouse, you should talk to your child about their reluctance, encourage your child to talk to the other parent about the situation, and continue to encourage time spent with both parents.

It is important for children to have a positive relationship with both parents and it will not get easier to build that relationship over time, therefore parents should do everything possible to build or maintain a good relationship with their child/children sooner rather than later.

Infants

Infants are likely to experience a feeling of loss of contact with their primary care-giving parent as well as the loss of their familiar and comfortable environment.

Symptoms may include depression, and/or regressing to an earlier stage of development. You may observe your child losing his or her ability to perform tasks and accomplishments he or she has already mastered.

Too long a separation from a child's primary caregiver may result in problems with separation and the ability to have healthy relationships later in his or her development. While brief periods of these types of behaviors and observations may not be serious, a sustained period may be cause for concern.

Children 3 -5 Years

Children 3 to 5 may regress to behaviors of earlier stages, such as bed-wetting, clinging or baby talk. The child may become more dependent, or withdraw into a fantasy world. Children may feel responsible for the divorce and may experience guilt. This may result in destructive, angry behaviors. Children may experience anxiety about basic needs such as food, shelter, and visitation. Children will often fantasize that their family has not separated and may hold onto hope that their parents will reunite. They may experience difficulties moving between households.

Risks associated with children experiencing divorce in this age group are that they may lose their ability to perform tasks they had already mastered; they may experience sadness, depression, low self-esteem, and feelings of abandonment; and they may carry power struggles, which are normal (during this stage), to later phases of development.

Children 6 -8 Years

Children this age tend to feel their anger and sadness more deeply. They may feel deprived, and may attempt to use food or material objects for their emotional needs. This age child has very strong loyalties, and may long for the non-custodial parent. These children may be more direct in their expression of pain and anger, and they may experience fears about money, food and housing. They fear losing both parents and may experience a great deal of self-blame about the divorce.

Areas of risk for these children include decreasing school achievement, long-term depression, preoccupation with the divorce, and inappropriate expression of hopes for reunion of their parents. Brief periods of regression are likely. Any sustained difficulties in school or changes in mood may need to be evaluated by a professional.

Children 9 -12 Years

This age child may be very angry at one parent. They may ask for details about the divorce. He or she may be aware of feelings of rejections and vulnerability and may experience sustained feelings of sadness, anger, and hurt. Children this age may also experience a sense of shame around their peers. They may seem to accept the divorce, but may be denying their true feelings.

Risks include:
> academic failures,
> lying,
> stealing,
> taking sides,

and feelings of
> loneliness,
> depression,
> and low self-esteem.

Children 13 -18 Years

Children this age may attempt to leave the family earlier than other children do. They may be unusually disappointed in one or both parents. They may place peer needs ahead of family, resulting in less interest in visiting.

Risks may include uncharacteristic use of drugs, sex, and/or religion to gain a sense of belonging to peer groups; somewhat delayed development, with a late approach to adolescence; and doubts about their own capacity to have a relationship. Other risks include, clinging to parents/family or withdrawing from them altogether.

CHAPTER 8

PARENTING TIME

Infants:

Short, frequent visits, no overnights. Keep to a routine. One home, one crib, one nighttime routine. Establish one primary residence.

Allow short, frequent stays of 1-4 hours with non-primary parent several times per week, increasing to 8 hours. No regular overnights at secondary home, unless in the company of an older child. Vacations with non-primary parent are not recommended until child nears two years of age, when periodic one or two night vacations may be considered.

Toddlers:

Can tolerate longer time away from primary care giver as toddlers can keep memory of the other parent; may introduce overnights. Increase length of daytime stays with non-primary parent gradually. As child nears three years of age, begin overnights once per week, increasing to two non-consecutive nights weekly, if parent has been highly involved. Periodic, half-week vacations with non-primary parent may be considered after age three.

Children 3-5 Years:

Alternate weeks or weekends for more equal time. Block of time with non-primary parent may increase from one to three overnights weekly. Begin to group two overnights together for older children. Some preschoolers do well with equal time-sharing, but many are still unable to handle separations, and overnights are inappropriate for those children. Frequent daylong visits may be more beneficial as often as they are possible. Periodic, weeklong vacations with the non-primary parent may be considered after age five.

Children 6-12 Years:

Longer time away from the parent who maintains the child's/children's legal (or the residential custodian), more equal sharing of time between households.

6-9 Years:

Equal time-share or near equal time-share works for many children. Weeks are best split in half, grouping the overnights together. Alternating weekends with mid-week daytime visits is still best for other aged children. Some children handle mid-week overnights well, but others find them disruptive. Two-week vacations with the non-primary parent may be considered after age seven, but only if weeklong vacations have been taken first.

9-12 Years:

Equal time with each parent benefits many children but can also be disruptive for many. One primary residence with evenings and weekend time-share for the non-primary parent is a pattern that often works. Mid-week overnights are successful for some children but not for others. Community and school activities must be maintained from both homes. Vacations longer than two weeks with the non-primary parent may be considered after age ten if child first has experienced a shorter vacation.

Teenagers:

More input, more flexibility; respect their wishes, encourage them to work out difficulties with other parent. Equal time-share is possible for some adolescents.

Alternating weeks may work. Other teens need a primary residence with evenings and some weekends spent in the non-primary parent's home. Vacations up to one month with either parent may be considered if shorter vacations have been taken. Once teens reach fifteen, vacations of more than a month can be considered, if they have been taking longer vacations up to this point.

Legal Considerations:

Be aware that our legal system is built off an adversarial model; therefore going to court to solve the problem will most likely:

- ❖ Exacerbate conflict
- ❖ Result in loss of time, energy, money, and control of confidentiality
- ❖ Result in fewer resources for children and self
- ❖ Allow for a third-party decision
- ❖ Keep you from seeking alternatives, such as mediation, arbitration, therapy, etc.

The legal system was not designed for domestic law, and therefore it tends to pit sides against one another. This model does not work well for parents who have to continue to co-parent and engage with one another after the divorce. This adversarial system tends to promote continued conflict. Mediation works off of a cooperative model that tends to help parents find compromise in their parenting plans and financial arrangements.

Reducing conflict in a divorce can save you time, energy, and money - all of which can be spent on yourself and your child/children. However, you should remember that it is common for both parents to feel that they have both lost financially, and also lost in regards to time with their child/children.

Rarely does either parent feel "victory" in a divorce.

Typically both parents will have less time with their children than before the divorce and they will also usually have fewer financial resources post-divorce.

Most parents going through divorce focus their energy on the first items in this list, however, better results will come from investing time, energy, and money into the bottom half.

- ❖ Legally Being Right / Being the Winner
- ❖ Financial Needs
- ❖ Support for family and self
- ❖ Learn better ways to communicate
- ❖ Understand children's experience
- ❖ Act differently; change your own behavior first

One of the most important things you can do is check and recheck your own behavior; your thoughts, your feelings, and your reactions.

PRACTICAL DO'S & DON'TS

- ❖ Do Stay Involved - Quality vs. Quantity.
- ❖ Don't interrogate your children about their other parent.
- ❖ Don't tell children secrets or expect them to keep secrets for you.
- ❖ Do attempt a smooth transition - not chaotic. No fighting in front of children.
- ❖ Don't use children as messengers.
- ❖ Don't let children decide entirely on their own where to live.
- ❖ Do discourage a child's reluctance to spend time with a parent.

It is possible to have a good divorce

CHAPTER 9

LEGAL TERMS

ALTERNATIVE DISPUTE RESOLUTION (ADR) - involves various methods of mediation, arbitration, or participation in settlement conferences that are designed to enable and empower parties to resolve their dispute without the need for formal court hearings or trials.

ARBITRATION - both parties agree to present their dispute to an independent, impartial arbitrator or panel of arbitrators who hear evidence and make decisions, as would a judge.

BEST INTEREST OF THE CHILDREN - basis upon which decisions are made about parenting time and custody. If parents are unable to agree on these matters then a judge will hear the case and make decisions based on what the judge believes to be the best interests of the children.

CHILD CUSTODY EVALUATIONS - an investigation done by court appointed mental health professional to determine what custody arrangement would be in the best interest of the minor children. The custody evaluation takes several months and includes clinical interviews, home visits, and psychological testing. At the conclusion of the investigation, the custody evaluator will write a report and file it with the court. Custody evaluations are ordered if either party requests one or if ordered by the judge.

CONTESTED HEARING - a contested hearing occurs when both parties are unable to agree concerning the issue of custody.

FAMILY COURT - created by the Fourth Judicial District to provide careful management of domestic cases.

GUARDIAN AD LITEM - an attorney appointed to represent the best interests of a child who is the subject of a custody proceeding. The Guardian ad litem is concerned with what custodial arrangement would best serve the interest of the child.

JOINT CUSTODY - refers to joint legal custody. Joint custody means that both parents remain in a decision-making capacity concerning their children. They are required to confer with one another concerning decisions of significance for their children and reach an agreement concerning such decisions whenever possible.

LEGAL CUSTODY - the right and obligation to make decisions for a child.

MEDIATION - a required meeting for parents to attend a session in the presence of an independent, trained and neutral third party called a mediator. The mediator assists the parties in reaching agreements on and concerning disputed matters including custody and parenting time.

PARENTING TIME - time a child spends with a parent.

PARENTING PLAN - a plan created by the parents for making decisions for their children, for resolving disputes, and to decide other matters inherent in the child rearing process.

PHYSICAL CUSTODY - refers to who has the child at any given time.

PRIMARY PHYSICAL CUSTODIAN - refers to whom the child lives, for a majority of the time.

RESIDENTIAL CUSTODY - the parent who maintains the child's legal residence.

SEPARATION AGREEMENT - a written document that sets forth all agreements reached by parties in their divorce case, including matters of child custody. A parenting plan may be included in a separation agreement.

It's about making this New Beginning for your children and you, the best it can be.

New Beginnings

KRISTINE TURNER

GUIDELINES FOR A
SUCCESSFUL PARTNERSHIP FOR PARENTING:

1. What you and your former spouse have as your mutual concern is the raising of your children. Make a conscious decision that you want to create a successful partnership for that project.

2. Be business-like with your former spouse in this partnership. Test all of your own behavior against this standard: Was I businesslike? Did I follow these guidelines?

3. Test your partner's behavior by the same standard - not by how you feel. Was your partner's behavior business-like? Did it conform to these guidelines?

4. Respect your children's relationship with your former spouse. Your children did not divorce either parent; do not force them to do so and encourage them to get over any feelings of estrangement they may feel about the other parent.

5. Make appointments to talk about business. Except for emergencies, call only during business hours or agreed upon times; always ask if the timing is convenient and if not, make an appointment for a time that is.

6. Be polite, do not use bad language or name-calling. Do not try to conduct business under the influence of alcohol or other drugs. If you feel yourself getting un-businesslike, say so and agree to resume the conversation later.

7. Give the benefit of the doubt as to behavior you would have with a stranger. Do not assume anything based on past experience without checking out current reasons for a behavior, what your former spouse thinks, or what your former spouse has decided.

8. Do not expect approval from your partner; get your personal and emotional needs met elsewhere and with others.

    On the other hand, if you are able to acknowledge something positive in word or deed toward your former spouse, do not withhold it. The reward of expressing appreciation, no matter how small, can be of greater success in the partnership.

9. Do not discuss what is irrelevant to business unless your former spouse specifically agrees otherwise.

    Respect your former spouse's privacy; do not seek to know the details of your former spouse's life and do not intrude on your former spouse's personal territory.

10. Make all agreements explicit and follow up with written confirmation when possible (or make your own written memorandum). Be clear and complete in communications; include time, place, whether children will be fed or not, what clothes they need, etc.

Communicate directly;
DO NOT ask the children
to do your business for you!

CHAPTER 10

RULES THAT FACILITATE COMMUNICATIONS

❖ No "zapping:, name-calling, or verbal slaps in the face.
❖ Own your own problem; use "I" messages (your feelings and opinions), not "you" (blaming) messages.
❖ Let the other person finish before you speak. Do not interrupt.
❖ No cross complaining. - If somebody complains to you do not answer with a com plaint.
❖ No bringing up the past, focus on the present and the future. It is unnecessary to discuss any-thing other than the very specific issue at hand when trying to co-parent. Outside issues muddy the waters and make co-parenting resolution much more difficult. Stick to the point.
❖ Stick to the topic, do not get sidetracked.
❖ Watch your effect and body messages; they should match what comes out of your mouth.
❖ Don't mind read.
❖ Restate the other person's comment specifically to the other person's satisfaction.
❖ If you are getting angry, tell the other person - withdraw and set up another time to continue the discussion.
❖ Be respectful.
❖ Deal with one issue at a time.
❖ Make requests not demands.
❖ Remember to listen, understand and acknowledge the other person's perspective. You do not have to necessarily agree.

COMMUNICATION TIPS

1. Attempt to achieve business-like, not emotional communications with your former spouse.
2. Try not to use terminal language like "never" and "always".
3. Does your behavior match your words?
4. Don't assume other's feelings.
5. Don't expect others to read your mind.
6. Reflect back to others what you think they are saying.
7. Avoid the "tit for tat" complaint responding.
8. Be polite.
9. Be specific.
10. Convert problems into goals for desired things.
11. Only discuss one issue at a time.
12. Pick a time and place to discuss issues.
13. Stick to the facts.

KRISTINE TURNER
OWNING YOUR OWN PROBLEMS:
"I" MESSAGES

Focus on your feelings and opinions, not blaming messages.

The "I" message gives you the control over what you are saying and doing. It makes you responsible for your words, actions, and emotions. By using "I" messages couples tend to avoid blaming and accusing the other parent for all the problems.

Use "I", not the word "you"
No name-calling
No "war-words"
No "never", "always", or "keep"

I feel _____
Because _____
And it matters to me because _____

The Solve Model

S   = Schedule a time to talk when both sides are calm.
O   = Outcome: each person specifies what he or she wants.
L   = Listening to each other's feelings and needs.
V   = Verbalize solutions that meet both people's needs.
E   = Evaluate. Set another time to review how well it is working.

The Happy Formula

H   = Help create security.
A   = Actively listen to your child.
P   = Provide rules and consistency.
P   = Protect your child from the painful conflict.
Y   = You commit to a better life.

Success Strategies for Parents

R   = Recognize the importance of meeting your needs.
E   = Establish a plan for creating your future.
B   = Build a working relationship with your co-parent.
U   = Understand that win-win solutions are possible.
I   = Improve your understanding of your child's needs.
L   = Learn and utilize the key ingredients for helping your child with the divorce.
D   = Divorce is both an ending and a beginning.

26

APPENDIX
OTHER RESOURCES

SUGGESTED READING
AND RESOURCE LIST

Books for Adults

- 101 Ways to Make Your Child Feel Special, Vicki Lansky
- 101 Ways to Be A Special Dad, Vicki Lansky
- 101 Ways to be a Special Mom, Vicki Lansky
- 101 Ways to Tell Your Child "I Love You", Vicki Lansky
- The Friendly Divorce Guidebook: Colorado, Wendy Whicher and M. Arden Haver
- Dance of Intimacy, Harriett Lerner
- Feeling Good, David Burns
- Getting the Love You Want: - A Guide For Couples, Harriett Hendrix
- Crazy Times, Surviving Divorce, A. Trafford
- How to Survive the Loss of a Love, Melba Colgrove, Harold H. Bloomfield, and Peter McWilliams
- Quality Time: Easing the Children through Divorce, Melvin Golzband
- The Divorce Experience, Morton M. and Bernice K. Hunt
- What Every Child Would Like Parents to Know About Divorce, Lee Salk
- Divorce: The Child's Point of View, Yvette Walozak and Sheila Burns
- The Survival Manual for Women in Divorce: 150 Questions and Answers, Carol Ann Wilson and Edwin Schilling
- The Custody Handbook, Persia Wooley
- Creative Survival for Single Mothers, Persia Wooley
- Families Apart: Ten Keys to Successful Co-Parenting, Melinda Bloau

Children's Books 3-6 Years Old

- ❖ Where is Daddy? Gaff
- ❖ Divorce Is... (Coloring Book), Magid and Schreibman
- ❖ Mom and Dad Don't Live Together Anymore, Shinson

Books for Children and Young Adults

- ❖ Mommy and Daddy Are Getting Divorced, Turner
- ❖ How to Get it Together When Your Parents are Coming Apart, Richard and Willis
- ❖ Surviving Your Parents' Divorce, Charles Boeckman
- ❖ Dinosaurs Divorce: A Guide for Changing Families, Laurene Brown and Marc Brown
- ❖ A Look at Divorce, Margaret S. Forria and Margaret S. Pursell
- ❖ Where in the World is the Perfect Family? Amy Heat
- ❖ How it Feels When Parents Divorce, Jill Krementz
- ❖ Why are we Getting a Divorce?, Peter Mayle and Arthur Robbins
- ❖ When Mom and Dad Divorce, Steven Nickman and Diane DeGoat
- ❖ It's Not the End of the World, Judy Blume

QUESTIONS:

1. What percentage of children currently live in a single parent home?
   a. 20%
   b. 30%
   c. 40%
   d. 50%

2. Currently, more people are part of a first marriage than a second or subsequent marriage.
   T or F

3. It IS possible to have had a bad marriage and still have a good divorce.
   T or F

4. When children are placed in the middle of divorce or are used as messengers, they may try to manipulate their parents
   T or F

5. You should try to ignore and downplay your emotional reaction to your divorce?
   T or F

6. Don't encourage children to explore their feelings about the divorce?
   T or F

7. Children can handle being placed in the middle of their parents divorce and they often make good go betweens if parents are having difficulty communicating?
   T or F

8. It is important to keep both parents involved?
   T or F

9. Which of the following are "predictors" of a "good" divorce?

Check all that apply.

a. Bad-mouthing the other parent in front of the kids.

b. Good conflict resolution

c. Putting yourself in your child/children's shoes.

d. Fighting when you see the other co-parent.

e. Listening actively to your child/children.

f. Thinking and acting like the family is broken and beyond repair.

10. Two of the most damaging results to children from a divorce are parental loss and parental conflict?

T or F

11. It is important to tell your child/children about the divorce. You should make sure to include which of the following point(s):

a. The divorce is final

b. The divorce is not the kids' fault

c. The divorce was an adult decision

d. All of the above

12. When parents say "Mommy and Daddy are getting a divorce because we fell out of love", children often worry that their parents could leave/divorce them or fall out of love with them?

T or F

13. In order to avoid parental loss, it is important to:

a. Limit travel out of town

b. Spend all your free time with your kids

c. Re-assure your child/children that you are available: (i.e. in person, by pager, via phone, e-mail, letters, etc.)

d. All of the above

14. What amount of time does the average parent spend "actively" listening to their child/children on a daily basis?

a. 20 minutes

b. 10 minutes

c. 5 minutes

d. 1 to 2 minutes

15. Children tend to identify with and understand themselves based upon who their parents are, therefore bad-mouthing the other parent when around the child/children often hurts the child more than the other parent.

    T or F

16. It's okay to depend upon your child/children for emotional support.

    T or F

17. Because children often grow up a little faster due to their parents' divorce, it is okay to "parentify" children.

    T or F

18. Children will tend to use their parents as a role model for how to emotionally manage the divorce.

    T or F

19. Children may try to get you to depend on them for support out of their fear of abandonment or parental loss.

    T or F

20. Which of the following are okay to discuss with your child/children?

    Check all that apply
    a. parental affairs
    b. your sadness
    c. your anger
    d. financial problems
    e. blaming the other parent
    f. your divorce

21. Which of these is NOT one of the five common stages of grief that you and your children and your former spouse go through during a divorce?

    Check all that apply
    a. anger
    b. bargaining
    c. denial
    d. relief
    e. acceptance
    f. depression

22. You will go through the five stages of grief at the same pace and time as your children and your former spouse.

T or F

23. Children will typically have a reaction to your divorce.

T or F

24. Which of these behaviors are NOT common reactions that children might express during a divorce?

a. regression
b. clinginess
c. fearfulness
d. emotional instability
e. relief
f. panic

25. Question: If your child/children are reluctant to spend time with you or your former spouse, you should:

a. Continue to encourage time spent with both parents.
b. Talk to your child/children about their reluctance to spend time with you or the other parent.
c. Encourage your child/children to talk to the other parent about the situation
d. All of the above

26. Mediators often achieve conflict resolution better for divorcing parents than attorneys because mediators tend to work off of cooperative models, whereas the legal system tends to be driven by an adversarial model.

T or F

27. It is common for both parents to feel that they have both lost financially, and also lost in regards to available time with their child/children.

Rarely does either parent feel "victory" in a divorce.

T or F

28. If your former spouse does something positive you should

a. acknowledge what has been said or done
b. ignore what he/she has said or done
c. downplay your former spouse's words or actions

29. Parents should try to communicate their emotions in co-parenting decisions with their former spouse.

    T or F

30. Which is not one of the five important aspects of the "SOLVE" model?
    a. verbalizing solutions
    b. scheduling
    c. evaluation
    d. victimization
    e. listening

31. It is helpful to bring up all the past issues when trying to settle a co-parenting issue about the children.

    T or F

32. The point of using "I" messages is to own your position or feelings about an issue.

    T or F

Kristine Turner, Ph.D.

558 Castle Pines Pkwy., Unit B4, #364

Castle Rock, CO 80108

Phone: 303.706.9424

Fax: 303.814.0365

Kristine.turner@NewBeginningsCoParenting.com

www.NewBeginningsCoParenting.com

PARALLEL PARENTING VS. CO-PARENTING

Parallel Parenting

1) Adult focused to avoid contact. Include the need for parents to disengage.

2) Parents speak only in emergencies and otherwise use email, text messaging or third parties (attorney, mediator or mutually agreed-upon person) to communicate.

3) Major decisions are "communicated" rather than discussed.

4) Households are separate. Each parent makes decisions about the child when the child is in their household.

5) Parents work separately for the best interest of the child.

6) Changes between households may be abrupt for the children. Use planned transitions to lower the anxiety of the exchanges.

7) Written parenting plan or court decree is followed exactly. Deviations from the parenting plan only offer opportunities for disagreement.

8) Each parent is responsible for their own relationship with child. The child is taught to differentiate between the different rules of the two households.

Co-Parenting

1) Focuses on the needs of the children.

2) Parents communicate regularly and use normal forms of communication such as face-to-face communication and phone conversations.

3) Major decisions about the child are discussed jointly

4) Parents work together as needed to resolve issues related to the child.

5) Parents work together in the best interests of the child.

6) Allows smooth transitions from one home to the other.

7) Allows for schedule change.

8) Parents may be able to discuss issues between other parent and child.

SECTION 2:

MOMMY & DADDY ARE GETTING DIVORCED

Helping Children Cope
With Divorce

Dedication

This book is dedicated to my children.

K.C. Conner, McKinzie, and Kylie,
you make life exciting
and new everyday.

Prologue

I was inspired to write this book years ago when I went through my own divorce. My children were young at the time, and I wanted them to have a book that dealt with the emotional aspects of divorce from a child's perspective. As a clinical psychologist in private practice since 1994, I decided that the best way to share my expertise as well as my experience with divorce was through books and seminars. This children's book gives both adults and children an overview of the normal feelings that accompany divorce and what to do with those powerful emotions.

There is a sadness in the house.

Mommy and Daddy are
getting a divorce.

That means that Daddy is going to have a home and Mommy is going to find a separate place to live. You and your brothers and/or sisters, if you have them, are probably going to live at both houses.

You will spend some of your time with Mommy and some of your time with Daddy. You may wonder what it will be like to live in two different places.

You may wonder if you will miss your Mommy when you are at Daddy's house. You may wonder if Daddy will miss you when you are at Mommy's house.

41

It might feel like it is too much to think about, and you may wish that you could just go to bed and forget about it.

You will have days when you want to wake up in the morning and have everything go back to the way it used to be before Daddy and Mommy decided to get divorced.

You may have thought to yourself, "If I wish really hard for this yucky feeling to go away, maybe it will be gone in the morning."

So, you go to sleep, but when you wake up the next morning, although it's a sunny day outside, you don't feel happy.

As a matter of fact, you feel weird inside. You can't believe that your life is going to change so much.

KRISTINE TURNER

You probably don't like when Mommy and Daddy fight, but you might want Daddy and Mommy to stay together and you might wish that life would feel "normal" again.

You may not like the change that is happening in your family. You may want to pretend that everything will go back to the way it used to be for you and your family.

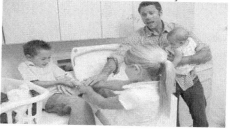

After a couple of months you might start to feel angry with your parents.

You might be mad at your Mommy for letting Daddy leave, or you might be mad at Daddy for getting a new home.

You might get mad at your friends; or get mad at your teachers, or even get mad at the dog.

You might feel mad about everything, but mostly you are angry because you can't bring your family back together. Your parents are going to get a divorce no matter how angry you get.

45

It may seem like you will never be happy again, and that you have no control over your life.

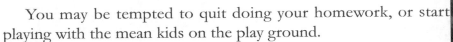

You may try being really bad to get the attention off of the divorce and onto yourself.

You may be tempted to quit doing your homework, or start playing with the mean kids on the play ground.

You may even get into a fight with your best friend, but no matter how many times your parents have to come talk to the teacher at school, they will still move forward with their divorce.

Sometimes kids try being really good.

You might try helping cook dinner, or taking out the trash, you might even volunteer to play with your younger sister, or brother, but no matter how good or how bad you are, nothing is going to put Mommy and Daddy back together again.

Your Mommy or Daddy might tell you that no matter how good or how bad you act, that Mommy and Daddy will always love you, but that they don't love each other anymore and that they have made an adult decision to get a divorce.

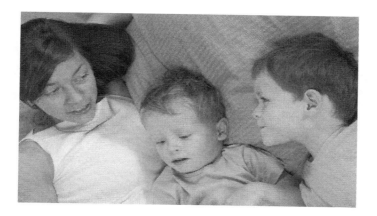

There is nothing you can do to change their minds. The divorce wasn't your fault, it was the adult's decision. You can't do anything to change the situation. Although you might feel disappointed, you will also realize that you have to get used to your parent's divorce.

At this point, you might start to feel really sad.

You might feel like you want to cry all the time. You will need someone to talk to about all the yucky emotions you are having inside.

Sometimes schools have teachers and counselors that can help you feel better.

These people will explain that many kids have families who are going through divorce.

The counselor might meet with you every week for a little while to talk about what it feels like to have your mommy and daddy go through a divorce.

A counselor or teacher may also say that it will help make you feel better if you talk about the sadness and the anger that you are feeling inside.

You might find that your grandmother, grandfather, or another family relative or coach may have more time to talk than your parents.

You might decide to talk to one of them about what has happened at school that day, or about how you feel about the divorce.

You might find that grandma is a good listener, and that she can talk about the yucky family stuff that is going on right now. As luck would have it, most grandmas and grandpas are good at listening, and they may tell you that you can talk to them any time you need to talk.

It will take time for things to feel better inside.

But as time goes by, you will start to feel normal again.

New
Beginnings

Mommy and Daddy are Getting Divorced

You will notice that your grades might get better in school again, you might start wanting to play with your friends again, you will start feeling happy again. You will also notice that your parents aren't fighting so much any more, and that the family seems to be getting used to living in two separate homes.

It won't be such a big deal if your parents run into each other at the store; and the little things won't seem to bug them so much anymore. Mommy will be happier in her new life, and Daddy will be happier in his life.

Slowly but surely, things will return to "normal" again. You will start to feel normal too.

Eventually, you will feel comfortable with the families' new situation.

Although it will have been a rough year or two, you will have learned that you have a strong family that can survive tough times.

You will also learn that it is important to talk about your feelings with other people when you are hurting inside. You will learn that many children go through divorce, and that there are a lot of adults who will help when times are rough.

Most of all, you will learn that if you work hard to get through something challenging you can succeed, and you can feel hopeful and happy again.

SECTION 3:

The Guide to a <u>Smart</u> Divorce

Experts' advice for
surviving divorce

by
The Divorce Team

Kristine Turner, Ph.D.
David W. Heckenbach, Esq.
Kurt Groesser, Realtor ®, MBA
Jan Parsons, Senior Mortgage Banker

DEDICATION

We dedicate this guide to those of you going through divorce. Although divorce can be difficult, it doesn't have to be devastating.

Many families grow and thrive during the divorce process. With the right information, you can manage your divorce successfully, grow from the experience, and achieve positive results.

May this information serve you and your family well.

Table of Contents

Foreword 60

Introduction: Your Options 61
    Pro Se
    Mediation
    Arbitration
    Rent A Judge
    Child and Family Investigator
    Parenting Coordinator and Decision Maker
    Collaborative Law
    Litigation

Legal Advice 66
    Dave's Personal Story
    So Many Lawyers, So Little Time
    Reputation is Golden
    Word of Mouth
    Published Resource Materials
    Hourly Rates
    Personalities
    Working with Your Attorney
    Cooperating with Your Attorney
    Using Discretion in Contacting Your Attorney
    Reasonableness

Finacial Advice 75
    My Role

Real Estate Advice 76
    Kurt's Personal Story
    Jan's Personal Story
    Should We Sell the Marital Home?

Tips for Selling Your Home Quickly
To Prepare Your Home for Sale
Hiring a Real Estate Agent
Questions to Ask Your Potential Real Estate Agent
Other Real Estate Assets
Capital Gains Taxes
Your Next Home
Think Before You Buy
Mortgage 101
Documents to Submit with Your Loan Application
Parts of Your Monthly Payment
Let's Talk Credit
What Your FICO Credit Score Means
Mortgage Products Available

Emotional Support and Parenting Plans 87
        Kristine's Personal Story
        Nobody Plans to Divorce
        Your Support System
        Telling Your Children About the Divorce
        Letting Your Children Express their Feelings
        Giving Your Children Routine and Consistency
        Fools Rush In
        Five Basic Emotional Stages
        Key Points to Remember
        Avoid Parental Loss
        Parenting Plans
        Parenting Classes
        Useful Tips to Help Your Children

About The Divorce Team 97

Resources 102

> *Throughout the book, you'll see these boxes and these are little stories from us or from clients we've served.*
>
> *These stories are the "I wish I'd have known..." real-life, 'learned the hard way' lessons that we hope we can spare all of you.*

Foreword

Divorce is difficult, but it
doesn't have to be devastating.

After having spent years working in the field of divorce, we of The Divorce Team collaborated to create this comprehensive yet easy-to-read guide for people going through divorce. If you are like most people, you did not plan to divorce and therefore are not prepared for the challenge. Divorce is a journey, and there are better and worse paths to take while moving through it. This guide is intended to help you think through the myriad of issues that arise and maneuver through your divorce effectively.

We are sure you have a number of questions about how to work through your divorce issues. Perhaps you need help with your parenting plan or you would like guidance on selling your house. Perhaps you need legal assistance or financial consultation. This guide was written in an easy-to-use format so that you can quickly get the information you need. You can also peruse other sections of this guide to help stimulate thinking around topics you may not have considered prior to filing for divorce.

This book was written with you in mind. We hope you find it helpful, and we wish you the best of luck getting through this transition in your life.

> *"The best thing I did for myself during the divorce process was to 'appreciate myself.' I actually thanked myself for working hard to have a positive divorce situation for my kids' sake and, in the end, it was for my sake, too."*

Introduction:

Your Options

Divorce is a major decision and a huge transition in life. Although it will undoubtedly be a lot of work to finalize your divorce settlement, the basic objective is to divide your assets and/or debt. If you have children, you will also need to provide a parenting plan for the courts to review. This divorce guide is designed to give you an overview of the divorce process, a few "tricks of the trade" and clarification on a variety of issues to help you determine the best course of action to finalize your divorce fairly and reasonably.

When you tell your family and friends that you have decided to get a divorce, they will do one or two of several things: say they are sorry, ask you why, try to talk you out of it, and give you unsolicited advice. They mean well, but at this point, you have already been through the heart-wrenching decision to get a divorce and are probably fairly confident you are doing the right thing. So although it is beneficial to have family and friends as part of your support system, they are not the best ones to approach for legal, financial, or even emotional advice.

What you need are professionals who know all the ins and outs of the divorce process, who have "been there, done that!" We of The Divorce Team are all experienced both professionally and personally in some or many aspects of divorce. In collaborating with one another on this book, we have learned that if we don't know something, we certainly know someone who does know or who can find out.

Your family and friends, even if they know a few things about divorce, are too close to you to be objective. What you need are professionals who understand that your divorce outcome will depend on a lot of variables, such as the divorce law where you live, current parenting trends, and what option you use to make your divorce legal.

You may think that there is only one means to this end, hiring an expensive attorney. But there is a continuum of options available for people going through divorce. Filing Pro Se is at one end of that continuum, while hiring an attorney to go to court for you is at the other end. The cost and the amount of time it will take to reach a settlement or agreement in your divorce will follow that same continuum. Typically, the more people you bring into your case, the longer it will take and the more it will cost. Before you spend a lot of time, energy, and money on your divorce, it's important to know what you are paying for and what you will likely get for your money.

PRO SE

About half the people going through divorce decide to file Pro Se. They file all of their own paperwork with the courts and they do it without any help from an attorney. If you file Pro Se you will be doing all of the work yourself. You can find all of the paperwork on court websites, and most courts have a Pro Se center where you can ask some questions about how to file everything properly. Some courts host classes or lunches where attorneys come and help you fill out your paperwork for free. If you can reach an agreement (settlement) on your own, it will be the least expensive, and it will set a precedence that demonstrates your ability to resolve your differences when they arise in the future. For example, if you have children, you are likely to have many discussions and decisions to make moving forward post decree (after your divorce is final).

MEDIATION

For the issues you can't resolve on your own, many courts will now mandate that you seek mediation before coming to court. You can choose to hire a mediator or the courts can appoint one for you.

A mediator acts as a neutral third party. They usually have a legal or mental health background and have been trained in mediation techniques. To resolve your differences, the mediator will work with you and your "spouse" either in the same office or separate rooms depending upon the level of conflict in your case. A mediator can work alone or you can bring your attorney(s) to mediation.

Your mediator will not decide your case for you; the decision-making power remains with you and your "spouse." Instead, a mediator will guide you in making reasonable decisions, for example, about the division of your assets and parenting plans (if you have children).

A mediator may help educate you about the process of divorce as well as remind you about all the details you will need to take care of or consider in your settlement, such as getting an appraisal on your house or splitting vacation time with the children. The beauty of mediation is that these decisions remain under your control. You don't turn them over to a third party.

ARBITRATION

If you opt for arbitration, it will play out like mediation but you will have given the arbitrator the decision-making power if you can't reach an agreement. In other words, if you can't finalize a settlement after meeting with the arbitrator for a couple of sessions, that person will put on a different hat, so to speak, and make the decision for you. Their decision becomes binding and gets filed with the court whether you like the decision or not.

RENT A JUDGE

Some couples find that they still want a judge to settle their differences, but they don't want to wait for the courts to hear their case. One option is to "rent a judge." Usually, your attorneys will represent you in a full blown hearing, but it will likely occur in a conference room versus a court room. You will also be paying the judge to attend the hearing, hence the term "rent a judge." As with arbitrator, the judge will make the decision for you and file it with the court.

CHILD AND FAMILY INVESTIGATOR*

If you are having trouble deciding upon a parenting plan for your children, you may want to hire a CFI (child and family investigator) to help you. This is usually a mental health professional who is also trained as a CFI.

This neutral third party will spend upwards of 40 hours meeting with your family, meeting with your children, and talking to your friends, neighbors, the grandparents, and/or children's teachers in order to make a determination as to the best parenting plan for your children. Note that the CFI will determine what is best for the children, not what is best for the parents.

A CFI can be very helpful in determining a parenting plan, but the process can be very difficult. For example, a CFI's report usually includes a personality assessment of both parents which can feel quite intrusive. You may struggle to present yourself in a positive manner during your evaluation when you are at your worst, not at your best. Then at a time that has probably made you feel vulnerable, it can be difficult to read the CFI's report section that indicates your strengths and weaknesses as a parent.

Although the CFI's report is only a recommendation on what you should do in regard to your parenting plan, it holds a lot of weight once it gets turned over to a judge or other decision maker. By hiring a CFI, you have turned some of the decision-making power over to a third party.

*This is the Colorado term. In other states, it may be called Custody or Parenting Time Evaluator or another name.

PARENTING COORDINATOR
AND DECISION MAKER

The PC/DM (parenting coordinator and decision maker) is another avenue to help you resolve disputes. These individuals are usually brought into a case post decree or after you have a settlement in place. Many people make the mistake of thinking that the divorce will end when they reach a settlement, file their paperwork with the court, and get their dissolution of marriage. However, you will likely find that you have to continue to interact with your former spouse if you have children. You will often need to make changes to your parenting plan throughout the years. This can be accomplished in all the previous methods above or through a PC/DM.

A PC/DM is usually a mental health or legal professional trained in PC/DM work. You will typically assign someone to your case; when an issue arises that you can't resolve, you will meet with your PC/DM to help you determine an agreement. Some PC/DM's will act more like mediators; others will have been given decision-making authority.

A typical case might go something like this: a couple has a parenting plan in place that says they each get two weeks of vacation with their children every summer. This works fine for the first two years, but in the third year, there's an overlap in their requests for vacation time. Mom wants to take the children to her sister's wedding in Hawaii at the same time Dad wants to take the kids to his family reunion in Maine.

If the parenting plan does not designate who gets priority vacation in odd or even years, the couple may come to an impasse. In this situation, they would call on their PC/DM to help them determine an agreement. If they cannot come to an agreement, the PC/DM will decide for them and enter the decision as a court order. In other words, the parents will lose their decision-making power if they can't make a decision together.

COLLABORATIVE LAW

Collaborative law is slightly different from hiring conventional family attorneys. In collaborative law, you and your "spouse" will agree ahead of time to hire collaborative law attorneys who will adhere to a specific collaborative process in reaching a settlement. You and your attorneys will attend negotiation meetings in conference rooms, the intent being to reach a settlement without going to court (litigation). However, if you can't reach a settlement and need to go to court, your collaborative law attorneys will resign from your case and you will need to start all over again with new legal counsel.

LITIGATION

Only about five percent of divorce cases actually go through litigation. Many more go through the process of preparing for it only to settle at the last minute to avoid the stress of litigation. It's not unusual for a case to resolve itself in the hallway of the court building right before it is to be heard by the judge.

To prepare for litigation, you and your "spouse" will hire your own attorneys who will take you through the process of discovery, which is sharing of all pertinent information related to finances and parenting. Then every effort is usually made to reach a settlement through avenues mentioned above, such as mediation and arbitration. The decisions that cannot be reached through negotiation are left to the courts.

Those include dividing property and debt, determining child and/or spousal support and sanctioning parenting plans. Your particular resolutions will depend on a combination of the laws of the state as well as the judges involved.

Bottom line: Not only does litigation leave important life decisions to the courts, but it is the most expensive and time-consuming means to an end, often taking up to a year to complete.

Whichever means you choose to legally dissolve your marriage and make decisions before and after your divorce, it is important to know all of your options. It is also important to let your family and friends know that this is your decision, just as getting a divorce is your decision. The more you are in charge, the better you will feel about the whole process, and the easier it will be.

**Remember, divorce is difficult but it
doesn't have to be devastating.**

LEGAL
ADVICE

DAVID W. HECKENBACH, ESQ.

Dave's Personal Story

I knew my divorce was coming. I knew it for months. I had been physically separated from my wife and had been "emotionally divorced" for some time. Yet when my wife filed for divorce, she exhibited a range of emotions indicating she was not at the same point. I felt helpless and worried about my relationship with our children. We went from contested court hearings at every stage and through multiple custody evaluations.

With the passage of time, however, we were able to put explosive acrimony aside for the sake of our children and also to preserve the quality of our own lives. It is with great gratitude I can say that I have enjoyed a healthy working relationship with my ex-wife for many years now. Never did our children flourish more than from the day their mother and I moved forward, forgave and placed their needs ahead of our own.

Today I tell my clients, "No matter how tough you think you are, no matter how emotionally prepared you believe you are, I can guarantee that you will not have anticipated all the negative emotions, the fears, the uncertainty, and the sense of loss and failure the divorce process generates." I am also able to tell them that they will be okay, there will be healing, there will be happiness and there can be a higher quality of life after divorce.

SO MANY LAWYERS,
SO LITTLE TIME

The divorce process can be simple and direct but many times it is not. When disputes regarding your children and their future arise, you want a competent lawyer at your side. When you consider that a divorce can be the single largest financial transaction of your adult life, you need an expert attorney to help you strategize. You will want to hire the best lawyer possible to achieve your goals over the course of the divorce process.

Almost everyone knows a divorce lawyer or someone who has gone through a divorce. There are many lawyers who claim to be qualified to handle even the most complex divorces. However, in my opinion, the number of truly competent family law practitioners makes up a small pool from which to draw. These attorneys place their clients' needs ahead of their own while having the experience, intelligence, and reputation that set them apart from the crowd.

REPUTATION IS GOLDEN

In your search for a good lawyer to help you through your divorce process, there are several precepts that should play into your decision. Most important, your lawyer needs to be respected in their community. No matter how much experience a lawyer has or claims to have, if they do not enjoy a good reputation for truth and veracity, competency and preparedness, they will not be well-received by the ultimate audience, the judge.

It is always preferable to settle a case rather than let the judge decide the fate of your children's future as well as your financial future. But in a small percentage of cases, judges must make the decisions. So although you should go into the process hoping for an expeditious and reasonable resolution, you should prepare for litigation before a judicial officer. If that judge does not know, does not respect or dislikes your attorney, you are disadvantaged.

Therefore, when you interview attorneys (and you should interview several), ask about their specific experiences in the jurisdiction in which your case will be filed, including their relationship with the judges and other judicial officers. An attorney can be imminently qualified with decades of experience, but if they are not known in your jurisdiction, it is a distinct possibility that the "good old boy" or "good old girl" on the other side will enjoy more positive results.

Bottom line: Make sure that your selection of an attorney is one who has specific experience and a solid reputation in your jurisdiction and with the judges who handle family law matters.

WORD OF MOUTH

An obvious resource to narrow your choice of attorneys is through those who have "been there, done that!" Don't just ask about their own divorce attorneys but about the attorneys on the other side. I am surprised by how many referrals I get from opposing parties who felt I did a good job and perhaps "out-lawyered" their own attorneys. And don't take the word of just one friend or family member. Just as you should interview several attorneys, you should talk to a variety of friends and associates.

PUBLISHED RESOURCE MATERIALS

There are a variety of published rating systems and distinctions that can be afforded practitioners. Probably the most notable resource is that of *Martindale-Hubbell* ® (www.Martindale.com), largely recognized for its peer-rating system. In order to achieve any sort of rating, an attorney must have been in practice for a certain number of years and meet minimum evaluative ethical criteria.

There are three general classes of ratings within *Martindale-Hubbell* ®. A-V is the highest, B-V is the next highest, followed by C-V. The "V" stands for "very" high ethical standards and the A, B, C standards are similar to grades you received in school. Attorneys who have achieved an A-V rating from *Martindale-Hubbell* ® are viewed by other lawyers and judges as highly ethical and very talented. That is not to say that you cannot find a good lawyer with either a B-V or even a C-V rating. It simply means that their peers familiar with their work believe them to be better or less so than other lawyers.

There is also an elite group of attorneys who first meet the criteria for an A-V rating and then are afforded the status of "Preeminent Lawyers." If you choose an attorney with an A-V Preeminent rating, you most likely have will have an attorney of extraordinary intellect, talent and skill.

While *Martindale-Hubbell* ® is probably the best known published resource, there are many others to help you in your selection of an attorney. An important one is membership in the local and/or national affiliate of the Academy of Matrimonial Attorneys (www.AAML.org). Although requirements for admission into these clubs vary from state to state, membership is generally restricted to those who limit their practices to family law.

One of the emerging arenas for attorney recognition is the "Super Lawyers" classification system, which, like *Martindale-Hubbell* ®, involves a listing of peer-rated attorneys who are in the top 5% of the lawyers practicing in their state. You can find this rating system at www.SuperLawyers.com.

There are any number of other groups, clubs and entities that either are or purport to be resource guides for the selection of an attorney but are too numerous to mention here. Regardless, your selection process circles back to finding a lawyer who is well respected, is smart, is a good strategist, and has significant experience with your type of case and in your specific jurisdiction.

A word of caution is in order. Exercise care and discernment when a lawyer holds themselves out as one with particular specializations. For example, there are a great number of lawyers that are qualified to assist fathers in exercising their rights; but if a lawyer is advertising as a "Father's Rights"

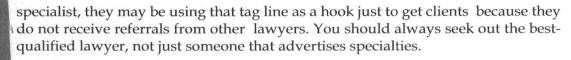

specialist, they may be using that tag line as a hook just to get clients because they do not receive referrals from other lawyers. You should always seek out the best-qualified lawyer, not just someone that advertises specialties.

HOURLY RATES

Hourly rates can fluctuate wildly, but generally speaking the more experienced lawyers, the busier lawyers and the lawyers that enjoy better reputations with the judges are going to cost more. That is not to say that you cannot find a very bright "up and comer" that does not charge an arm-and-a-leg. After all, the "old dogs" that are charging significant hourly rates were once in that category at some point in their careers.

One of the most common questions I get during initial consultation is "How much will this cost?" After 31 years of practice, many as a family law practitioner, I have yet to come up with a good answer to this question. There are far too many variables. Even if you were the most reasonable, manageable, empathetic client, it is impossible to control the behavior of the other side.

Of the four people typically involved in a divorce, the two parties and their respective attorneys, it only takes one to make the process thorny, protracted and expensive for all concerned. The amount your case will cost is directly proportionate to the amount of disagreement there arises between you and your "spouse." Because emotions are almost always raw, there are usually more problems than initially anticipated.

Another factor to consider is efficiency. An attorney who charges $500 per hour may very well be able to accomplish in three hours what takes the $250-per-hour attorney ten hours to do. There are always tradeoffs.

In my firm as in most, we assign a task to the person with the lowest hourly rate capable of a particular service. For example, organization of discovery documents is performed by a paralegal; research and motion drafting is done by a mid-level or even beginning associate; and trial strategies and the trial itself are conducted by a senior attorney. This is not the case should you choose a solo practitioner who in the end may cost you more because they charge every detail at their hourly rate.

Therefore, it is not necessarily wise to make your choice of attorney based on hourly rates alone. If an attorney enjoys a good reputation and is part of a reliable firm, although expensive, they may end up costing you less than a cheaper attorney with a bad or no reputation who is working on their own.

PERSONALITIES

As with any group of professionals, lawyers have different personalities. Some are more empathetic than others; some are better communicators than others; and some are more cut-throat than others. The critical component with picking a personality is that you as the client have a high level of comfort as well as confidence in who you have selected. Divorce is often a terribly emotional experience. The fear of the unknown with respect to your children and your financial future can be overwhelming.

Therefore, you should always interview several lawyers that meet your criteria in terms of experience and reputation to ensure your comfort level with the one you ultimately choose. On paper, you might have three lawyers with virtually identical qualifications, years of experience and reputation, yet you may find they have three distinct personalities.

Hopefully, you will feel comfortable with at least one of the attorneys you have chosen to interview. But if you don't, you can widen your search until you find the perfect fit for you. You don't want to be switching lawyers in midstream. When a judge sees a client who has changed attorneys two or more times during their divorce, they understandably come to believe that the client is the one who is unreasonable rather than the other side. That is not to say that your initial decision may not be the right one for you. But without a substantial reason for changing counsel, it is rarely a good idea to do so.

Therefore, it is important to make the best choice possible according to recommendations, ratings, reputations, and your own gut instinct. In the end, go with the most qualified attorney with whom you feel the highest level of comfort and personal rapport. Divorce is too difficult a process to go through with someone you dislike. While you may not become best friends with your attorney, it is necessary to have a collaborative and respectful relationship.

WORKING WITH
YOUR ATTORNEY

If you have decided to be represented in your divorce by an attorney, there will be a cost, no doubt. But the amount of that cost is in part attributable to your conduct and behavior throughout the course of the process. As noted previously, the more disagreement, the more expense. And while it only takes one person involved to run costs up for everyone, there are ways to contain the amount of your attorney's bill.

Further, there are ways to contain and define the range of risks with which you engage during the divorce process. A saying I share with most of my clients is that two experienced attorneys with two reasonable clients can carve up a marital estate with a scalpel in a way that healing can begin quickly. In contrast, allowing a judge to decide your case is similar to sitting in the front row of the comedian Gallagher's show where he takes a sledge hammer and smashes the watermelon (your marital estate) and whatever sticks to you, you keep, whatever sticks to your "spouse," they keep.

Clearly, it is not always possible to settle cases. Sometimes there are disputes with regard to the welfare of children that have the parties so polarized the judge must make the decision. When there are substantial disagreements regarding the marital character of assets or the amount of spousal support, litigation may be the only way to resolve the case. But if at all possible, both parties should make every reasonable attempt to settle the case out of court. To that end, you can only control your side of things. By acting in good faith, you will do all you can to help minimize your cost.

COOPERATING WITH
YOUR ATTORNEY

Divorce entails sharing a great deal of information with each side. You and your "spouse" will be required to exchange all pertinent financial information and all materials regarding minor children. There are basically two ways to proceed with this process. The first is to make every effort to assemble your documents in an organized fashion for your attorney. Otherwise you will have to pay for your attorney's staff to hunt for, sort through and identify pertinent documents.

The second and less intelligent way is to play games by attempting to hide money/assets or delaying your response to requests for obligatory and mandated disclosures and discovery. If you do not comply, you will end up paying your attorney or the other side's for their time spent playing your game. One way or the other, the necessary information will be obtained because it is your attorney's ethical charge to produce it. The higher your level of cooperation with this endeavor, the less expensive it will be for you.

New
Beginnings

USING DISCRETION IN
CONTACTING
YOUR ATTORNEY

Using discretion in contacting your attorney can be difficult. Emotions are running at their peak and even the slightest perceived infraction by the other side can spark tremendous anger and frustration. Calling or emailing your attorney each time your spouse has the children back seven minutes late will cost just as much as calling or sending an email about the $500,000 disparity between your expert's business evaluation and the other side's.

While you should never hesitate to contact your attorney about matters of importance, you need to let a little bit of time pass before reacting and contacting your attorney over issues that will not make a material difference in your case. If anything, keep a journal or a log, but do not waste your money and your attorney's time on minor issues that will not affect the outcome of your divorce.

REASONABLENESS

It is important to recognize and accept that this is going to be a highly charged emotional time for you and your "spouse." There are feelings of betrayal, anger, mistrust and frustration in nearly every divorce proceeding. Pride, "the principle of the thing" and "money to spend" are your lawyer's meal tickets and they will lead to issues and asset depletion that you will regret in the not-so-distant future.

And while recognizing that the other side may be petty, malicious or vindictive, you have little chance of changing their behavior. You probably couldn't control their behavior during the marriage, so you certainly can't now. All you can do is control your side of things.

That is not to say that it is inappropriate to react in a legal and measured way when your spouse violates court orders or fails to properly disclose assets that are to be divided. Rather, it is up to you to make every effort to behave reasonably, to listen to the advice of the attorney you have chosen. The more reasonable, candid, and cooperative you are, the more effective your lawyer can be and the less expensive your divorce will be.

While it is unwritten, most divorce practitioners recognize what we have affectionately come to call the "Son-of-a-Bitch Rule." Attorneys and clients that underestimate this rule find themselves walking out the courtroom with their tail between their legs, feeling hammered by the presiding judicial officer.

This rule is simple: judges are human beings. Even in a "no fault" state, if they perceive that one of the parties has behaved badly during the course of the divorce, if that person has been deceitful, tried to hide assets, or in any way been unreasonable, the judge may make them pay dearly.

Plus judges in domestic cases have wide latitude; it is extremely difficult to get such cases reversed on appeal because the legal standard is whether or not there is evidence in the record to support the judge's findings or if the judge abused their discretion in entering the orders. The appellate court will not substitute its personal judgment for that of a trial judge.

No matter what, if you have to litigate your case you do not want to be perceived as the "Son of a Bitch" that will one way or the other be punished by the judge. Therefore, if your attorney tells you that the judge won't appreciate what you are trying to do, listen. As a litigator, nothing suits me more than walking into a courtroom with a client who has been reasonable when the other side has not played by the rules.

Playing games results in loosing discretionary calls to the other side at the hands of the judge as well as increased costs, perhaps even being sanctioned to pay the other side's attorney fees. Behaving reasonably, cooperatively and decently keeps your costs down and maximizes your position in front of the judge.

"I kept wanting to make my former spouse pay for the hurt and pain she had caused me, and I wanted to minimize her child support and maintenance in order to do this. It wasn't until three years post divorce and a number of nasty trips to court that I realized that no matter how much I did or didn't have to pay her, it would never heal the wounds inside of me. I had to heal these emotional injuries in a healthy way. I had to overcome my own hurt and pain irrespective of how she chose to live her life."

FINANCIAL ADVICE

<u>My Role</u>

Realizing through my own personal experience that the traditional divorce process can fall well short of identifying financial scenarios that can lead to a more equitable result, I proudly embrace the skills and tools that Certified Divorce Financial Analyst® designation provides,

My role is to help both client and lawyer understand how the financial decisions made today will impact the client's financial future, based on certain assumptions.

A CDFA™ may come from a financial planning, accounting or legal background, and goes through an intensive training program with the goal of becoming skilled in analyzing and providing experience related to the financial issues of divorce.

A CDFA™ becomes a part of the divorce team, providing support for the lawyer and client, or becomes a member of a Collaborative Law team. In either event, the CDFA™ will be responsible for:

- Identifying the potential short-term and long-term effects of dividing property.
- Integrating tax planning strategies.
- Analyzing pension and retirement plan issues.
- Helping the client determine if they can afford the matrimonial home – and if not, what might be an affordable alternative.
- Evaluating the client's insurance needs.
- Establishing assumptions for projecting inflation and rates of return.
- Bringing an innovative and creative approach to financial planning solutions.

REAL ESTATE
ADVICE

KURT GROESSER,
REALTOR ®, MBA

JAN PARSONS
SENIOR MORTGAGE BANKER

Kurt's Personal Story

In the summer of 1984, my parents decided on a trial separation and began divorce proceedings. My sister was thirteen years old and I was only seven, but I still have vivid memories of moving out of our home on Buttonwood Drive. My parents had been fighting for months and, in many ways, I was relieved to be in a new environment.

It was a small two-bedroom townhome on Strachan Drive and my father, sister, and I quickly made it our home. My sister and I still call it "the Strachan House" when we talk about that time. The floor plan was much smaller than our Buttonwood home and the yard was a postage stamp, but that didn't stop me from running around the small yard emulating the Olympians we watched in the summer games that year.

My father is a proud man and I have little doubt that renting "the Strachan House" after years of home ownership played on his ego. We were downsizing but we were regrouping—emotionally and financially. We lived there for a year before we settled again in a new home.

Ultimately, it didn't matter to my sister and me that we were living in a rental home. We just wanted things to get back to normal. Summer turned to fall and I enrolled in a new elementary school and found new friends. Our family survived and, fortunately, my parents were able to reconcile their differences that year without finalizing the divorce. I look back on that time at "the Strachan House" with a sense of great strength even though it was difficult.

I share this story with you for two reasons. First, don't assume that you have to immediately provide a "worthy replacement" to the marital home you and your children have known. Second, what your children need most is a sense of normalcy, and a transition home, like our "Strachan House," may be the best way to facilitate that.

Jan's Personal Story

After I divorced, I thought I needed to keep my son in the same type of neighborhood we were moving from—large upper-middle-class homes in nice, tidy cul-de-sac's. I immediately jumped into a new, large house with a big backyard. Even though my brother encouraged me NOT to purchase the new house, I was singing "I am Woman, hear me roar!" But I jumped right into the proverbial frying pan.

What I have learned in the last few years is that my dog, Hannah, large as she may be, is a house dog who loves being indoors with her family. My son LOVED living at his father's small, rented condominium. I, on the other hand, did NOT love caring for a large house and yard. I was incapable of giving my undivided attention to my son on the weekends because I was busy mowing, edging, weed-eating and cleaning.

After about a year of keeping up the maintenance, I was yearning for a nice smaller-sized townhome where someone else took care of the landscaping and snow blowing and I could concentrate on soccer and basketball with my son.

I also took out a large mortgage on my new home thinking that when I started back into the business world I would be hugely successful. What I failed to remember was that I had not worked in seven years and it was a bit more difficult getting back on my feet than I had anticipated. Not only was I yearning for a smaller home, but also a smaller mortgage.

By all means, if you have the financial strength to purchase the Taj Majal and hire a gardener and cleaning person, you have my blessing. But if you have an uncertain financial future like I had, it is best to play it safe. I now wish I had rented for a few months until my head was clear and I was thinking more logically instead of emotionally.

Should We Sell the "Marital Home"?

For most couples, the marital home is the most significant financial burden as well as the most significant asset in their portfolio. The decision to sell or not to sell can be an emotional rollercoaster and the main battleground in the divorce. In some situations, the divorce proceedings may require the sale of the home in order to divide the proceeds equitably. If neither spouse can afford to keep up the house payments alone, it will be in their best interest to sell as quickly as possible. Couples with children will have other considerations, such as whether or not to keep the home until the children finish school.

One of the first things you can do to help make your decision is to get an appraisal. Although many popular websites will offer an estimated value of your home, the information is often not accurate. Neither do you want to rely on the tax assessor's value of your home. Instead, get a Broker's Opinion of Value (BOV) or a Comparative Marketing Analysis (CMA) from a local real estate agent. Your attorney along with any professional involved in your divorce will need to get this information.

Keep in mind, the value of a house is ultimately determined by what a buyer is willing to pay for it and what you are willing to sell it for TODAY. Unfortunately, many people have preconceived notions of what their home is worth based on the "real estate bubble" in the mid to late 2000's. If you were not fortunate enough to sell your last home at its artificial peak during that time or if you bought your current home during that time, you may have lost some of your equity during the market correction. In order to sell your home as quickly as possible for the best price, you will need to know what the home is worth NOW.

If your home is worth less than what you currently owe, you have several options. First, one spouse may be able to keep the home until the market improves. Second, a loan modification may lower the payment to a manageable level. Third, you can rent the home until the market improves. Fourth, you may be able to negotiate a short sale of the home. In a short sale, a real estate agent will list your home for sale and market it to buyers just as they would in a normal sale. Once you receive an offer, the agent will negotiate a settlement with your bank to forgive the short fall or arrange for a reduced payment to settle the remaining debt. A short sale has important tax and legal consequences to the divorcing couple, so you will need to discuss this option carefully with both your CPA and attorney.

Tips for Selling Your Home Quickly

The moment you place your home on the market you are entering a competition—a price war and a beauty contest. Winning homes will have the best value in both of these categories in the eyes of buyers. One of the most important questions you need to ask your realtor is: "How do we stack up against the competition?" Investors who regularly fix up and sell houses will make sure their properties have better curb appeal and more "bang for the buck" than comparable homes. A few things you can do include clearing the clutter, touching up paint, and hiring a realtor who uses a professional photographer.

TO PREPARE YOUR HOME FOR SALE

❖ Clean up the clutter, especially in the bathrooms and kitchen (remove unnecessary items and appliances from the countertops)

❖ Hire a handyman to finish projects and/or touch up paint inside and outside

❖ Have carpets and windows cleaned

❖ Hire a professional home stager

❖ Make sure your real estate agent uses a professional photographer for marketing

What do you do if your "spouse" does not comply? Unfortunately, it is quite common to have one spouse sabotage the efforts to sell the marital home. The courts can help to resolve disputes over the showing and staging of the home. If your soon-to-be-ex is causing problems with scheduled showings or leaving the home in disarray, talk to your attorney right away. You cannot afford to miss out on a buyer who is ready, willing and able to buy your home.

HIRING A REAL ESTATE AGENT

You've made the difficult decision to sell the marital home; now it's time to pick the best real estate agent to sell it quickly for the best price possible. So who do you choose? Most of us know a friend, family member or acquaintance who "dabbles" in real estate, but if you want to make sure your home sells quickly this is NOT the time to hire your friend's mother's cousin to list your home. An experienced agent who knows the current economic situation and consistently sells homes faster than the average for your area is your best option.

Professional real estate agents will often be a member of the local board of Realtors® and will have access to marketing your property on the local board website, often called the MLS (multiple listing service). You will also want to consider interviewing several agents who have successfully sold homes in your neighborhood.

You may want to hire an agent who specializes in divorce (www.RealEstateDivorceSpecialist.com). Divorce proceedings can complicate the sale of a house if there are disagreements over the distribution of the marital assets or liens placed on the property. If you can't successfully complete the sale of your home after you've gone under contract with a buyer, the legal and financial ramifications could be very costly, depending on the laws in your state.

There are several questions to ask an agent when interviewing one to list your home, including if they work full-time, how long their houses are on the market, on average, and what do they do to market homes. If you and your "spouse" can't agree on a real estate agent, the courts may select one for you.

QUESTIONS TO ASK YOUR POTENTIAL REAL ESTATE AGENT

❖ Are you a full-time or part-time agent?
❖ What is the average number of days your listings are on the market before selling?
❖ What websites will my home be listed on?
❖ How quickly do you respond to phone calls?
❖ How often can I expect to hear from you concerning updates?
❖ What specifically do you do to market properties?

"I had previously been the sole owner of my home prior to my marriage. Upon divorce, I didn't realize that I only had to include the amount that the house had increased in value since the marriage as a 'marital asset.' I was so relieved to learn that this was the only part of the home that he was entitled to in the divorce."

OTHER REAL ESTATE ASSETS

Investment properties are important to consider in the division of marital assets. They may be rental property, vacation homes, time shares, or commercial real estate investments. The factors that distinguish an investment from a personal residence are related to ownership and use. If either spouse used the property as a personal residence in two of the last five years, the property may be considered a personal residence eligible for an exemption from capital gains taxes. On the other hand, investment properties are generally subject to capital gains taxes when sold. You will want to talk to your CPA and real estate agent about the benefits of a 1031 Exchange to defer your capital gains tax burden and roll your equity into a new investment property (see more on capital gains rules below).

Keep in mind that a property deeded in one person's name can be sold prior to the divorce proceedings without the consent of the other spouse. After the divorce begins, the courts may issue an injunction that prevents the sale of properties while the divorce is proceeding. Also, a "lis pendens" order may be used to further diminish the chances of a spouse selling a property during a divorce. The order is publicly recorded with the county and indicates to any prospective buyer that there is a court proceeding that could prevent the clean sale of the property while the title to the property is "clouded." A "lis pendens" is very effective but it also requires a court order to be removed; you will not be able to sell the property until it is fully removed from the title.

Depending on the laws of your state, there may be specific rules that dictate the division of marital property. Marital property refers to any property purchased by either spouse during the marriage up to the time of the final divorce decree. Property that was inherited or gifted to either spouse and held in separate title is treated differently. In many cases, the appreciation in value of properties from the time they were received is considered marital property. Properties owned by a spouse's business might also be considered marital property.

It may not be necessary to sell all (or any) of the marital properties to divide real estate assets. In fact, if the properties are appreciating in value, it may be beneficial to keep the properties until they achieve a higher value. Properties can be deeded from one spouse to another with a "quit claim deed" by a lawyer or title company. This transfer is a quick and relatively simple way to divide the marital property and it has no tax consequence to either spouse. When a property is later sold, however, it will likely be subject to capital gains taxes. Be sure to talk to a CPA and financial planner about the latest tax rules relating to the sale of investment properties.

CAPITAL GAINS TAXES

Over the years the US Tax code has allowed homeowners to waive a portion of their capital gains on the value of their personal residences. In order for a home to be considered a personal residence, there are ownership and use criteria that must be satisfied. As of 2010, your home is considered a personal residence if you have owned it for at least five years and have used it as your home address for at least two of those years. Currently, married couples are eligible to use a $500,000 capital gains tax exemption on the sale of a personal residence. Single people are eligible for a $250,000 capital gains tax exemption.

For a divorced couple, there are special rules that allow both spouses to individually receive the $250,000 tax exemption on their marital home, even years after the fact. If your "spouse" received the home in the divorce settlement, you may still qualify for the exemption once the home is sold. To be eligible, however, you will need to remain on the title to the home, so plan carefully at the start of the divorce. Either party can use their "spouse's" use of the home for two of five years for the eligibility requirement. Obviously, this can be complicated, so you will want to consult with a lawyer, financial planner, and CPA to set the scenario up correctly from the start.

YOUR NEXT HOME

The divorce is final, the marital home has sold and you are left to decide whether to purchase a home or rent. First, DO NOT compete with your "spouse." Don't give in to perceived pressure from your children or elsewhere to replace the big house. Next, don't make competitive jabs in the years after the divorce by trying to outdo your "spouse" with homes and/or property. Instead, talk to a financial planner to develop a new vision to achieve your personal goals and use that plan to direct your decisions. A costly real estate mistake can be difficult to undo.

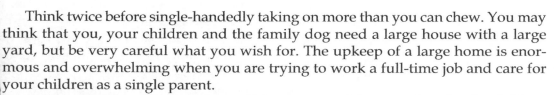

Think Before You Buy

Think twice before single-handedly taking on more than you can chew. You may think that you, your children and the family dog need a large house with a large yard, but be very careful what you wish for. The upkeep of a large home is enormous and overwhelming when you are trying to work a full-time job and care for your children as a single parent.

If the marital home has not been sold, you may wish to stay in it for the children or yourself. This may be a wise decision if you can financially accomplish it. However, it will need to be refinanced if both you and your "spouse" are on the note and/or loan. Your income will likely be cut so you should consult a mortgage professional to find out if refinancing is feasible.

You may be surprised what a mortgage professional can do for you. You may qualify for a loan when you don't have much to put down, which is preferable to renting for a long period of time. Or you may need expert testimony in court stating you can afford to refinance on your own and buyout your "spouse." Bottom line: Contact a mortgage professional to see what options are out there now or in your future with proper planning.

Mortgage 101

You have found a new home or possibly a vacation home in the mountains or near the ocean. Perhaps you would like to own investment property and become a landlord. These are all different types of properties and the interest rates will vary according.

Let's start with your primary residence. Before you begin shopping for a new home, it is important to contact a mortgage professional to both know what price range you can afford and get pre-qualified. Keep in mind that getting pre-qualified does not mean that you will absolutely qualify. It just means that you have gone through the preliminary stages of the pre-qualification process. You have been pre-qualified, NOT pre-approved.

A loan officer will ask you several questions. A main one: "What does your credit look like?" Have a copy of your credit report handy so you are familiar with your credit score as well as what debt shows on your report. Another question: "What is your income?" Know your earnings, either annually or monthly. Next: "What are your assets?" These include a 401K, an IRA, stocks, etc.

Also, if you either receive or pay child or spousal support, you must disclose this to your loan officer. Your divorce decree must state that you will be receiving child/spousal support for at least three years for a lender to accept it as income.

Your mortgage professional will also need to know how much you plan on putting down and how long you plan on living in your new home. Perhaps this is a transitional home or maybe it is the home you plan on never leaving. Once your loan officer has all your information and has discussed your long-term financial goals, they will go to work to see if you qualify to purchase a home. There are several different loan programs and they should be willing to show you all your options.

Once your loan officer has determined the price range you can afford and has you pre-qualified, the fun begins. It's time to call your real estate agent. It's also time to introduce your mortgage professional to your agent. They will be working together. Your realtor will need to ask your loan officer for a "pre-approval letter." This basically states that you have been pre-qualified for a loan in a certain price range. When you find a home and make an offer, this document will be given to the listing realtor. When your offer gets accepted, you and your loan officer will get to work to obtain a mortgage. There are some basic documents they will need from you such as a copy of your driver's license, pay stubs and a divorce decree, among many others. They will submit these with your loan application.

DOCUMENTS TO SUBMIT WITH YOUR LOAN APPLICATION

❖ Signed purchase contract

❖ Copy of your driver's license and Social Security card

❖ Evidence that you are obtaining homeowner's insurance

❖ Signed loan documents (your lender will prepare these once you have a contract on your home)

❖ W-2's or tax returns if you are self-employed

❖ Pay stubs

❖ Checking and savings account statements

❖ Asset statements

❖ Divorce decree if applicable

Parts of Your Monthly Payment

PITI: Principal, interest, taxes and insurance

Principle: The overall principle is the amount you borrowed and are charged interest on. The monthly principle is the amount actually being deducted from the overall principle. This amount goes up over time.

Interest: The overall interest is the amount that borrowing the principle is costing you (along with the loan fees). The monthly interest is the interest cost for that month. This amount goes down over time.

Taxes: Property taxes vary according to the county you live in and are determined monthly by dividing your annual assessment by twelve months.

Insurance: The mortgage lender will require you to obtain homeowner's insurance to cover your home against theft, fire and natural disasters.

HOA Dues: HOA (home owner's association) dues will not become part of your mortgage payment, but the monthly amount will be included to ensure you can pay your HOA dues.

LET'S TALK CREDIT

Your credit score and debt are important pieces to a complicated puzzle. A potential lender will need to pull your credit from three different credit reporting bureaus. Most often, your "mid-FICO* score" is what determines your interest rate along with qualifying you for a loan: the higher the score, the better the interest rate. It's a good idea to obtain your own credit score first so you can correct any inaccuracies. It's not uncommon for there to be errors.

It's also not a bad thing to carry some debt. The rule of thumb is to not have more than 30% of your available credit charged on any loan. Keep to that and make your payments on time and your credit should stay in good shape.

WHAT YOUR FICO CREDIT SCORE MEANS

If your score is less than 620, you currently will not be pre-approved for a home mortgage.

If your score is 620 to 680, you may qualify for an FHA loan.

If your score is 680 and above, you may qualify for a conventional loan.

If your score is 720 and above, you will qualify for a loan with the best rates available at that time

Negative factors that may have lowered your FICO credit score include closing accounts, moving often, high balance on credit cards and charge-offs. If your credit is not in the best shape, do not despair. It is always repairable. Your mortgage professional should be able to guide you in the right direction for improving your credit score.

> *"The best advice I got during my divorce was to take the high road, grin and bare it and never badmouth my former spouse. This has paid off in spades. It kept me from exposing my 'dirty laundry' to the neighborhood, and it kept my children safe from nasty comments and discussions about their parents' divorce. It also made it easier to eventually be friendly with my ex."*

* FICO stands for Fair, Isaac and Company, the company that historically assigned credit ratings.

MORTGAGE PRODUCTS AVAILABLE

30-YEAR FIXED:

The 30-year fixed mortgage is the most common product out there today. With this type of mortgage, your loan will stay unchanged throughout the life of the loan. If you plan on living in your home for many years, this is your bet.

ADJUSTABLE-RATE MORTGAGE:

With an adjustable-rate mortgage, the interest rate will vary depending on if you choose a three, five, seven or ten-year adjustable-rate mortgage. The interest rate will be lower than a 30-year fixed loan, but it will adjust when your term is up. This product works if you know you will only be in your home for three to ten years. Let's say you have a daughter who is in tenth grade and will be graduating in two years and going away to college. Perhaps you will want to downsize then or retire near your family. This product makes good financial sense if you are CERTAIN you will be selling soon. But you don't want to get stuck with a higher interest rate should you stay.

FHA (Federal Housing Administration):

If you have a minimal amount of savings for a down payment, an FHA loan is the product for you. You can choose from a 30-year fixed or an adjustable-rate mortgage. An FHA loan also allows for a less-than-stellar credit score. As long as you have a 620 mid-FICO score or higher, FHA is willing to lend to you.

Current guidelines require you put down 3.5% of the purchase price. You will also need mortgage insurance which helps guarantee your repayment of the loan. If you do not have 3.5% to put down on a home, there are several "down payment assistance programs." Some require as little as $500 down and many will defer the payments for several years and or have very low interest rates attached to them.

❖   ❖   ❖

Bottom line: Consult with your mortgage professional to find a program that fits your needs. The process of obtaining a mortgage may seem a bit intimidating, but it is well worth the outcome once you are given the keys to YOUR new home.

> *"My best support systems were my closest friends and family members. I was careful not to rely on my children for support. I had watched my neighbor depend on her kids for emotional support during her divorce and her kids were practically raising her."*

EMOTIONAL SUPPORT
AND
PARENTING PLANS

KRISTINE TURNER, PH.D.

Kristine's Personal Story

I went to graduate school, got my degree as a clinical psychologist, got married, bought a house, and had children in my twenties. In my thirties, I unexpectedly got a divorce. I mistakenly believed that my years of experience as a psychologist and facilitator of parenting after divorce classes would make the process easier. Unfortunately, I forgot to calculate the depth of emotional factors that would play into the whole ordeal.

Initially, I thought we could settle the divorce in an amicable manner. After a few failed attempts, it became clear that both of us would need to hire attorneys to help us through the process. I didn't interview attorneys, which was a big mistake, going with the first one someone recommended. I didn't like working with her and dreaded every interaction we had, not to mention paying the bill each month.

As the case wore on, I became physically and emotionally exhausted. Although divorce was our solution to the marital problems, it became a problem unto itself. The more time we spent with attorneys, the less we talked to each other, and the more we came to distrust and dislike the other person. Neither of us was getting our needs met, and both of us were fostering a "fear factor."

Our limited conversations left us frustrated and hurt and we lacked the tools to reach a settlement on our own. If we had been forced into mediation, as many states now require, we might have resolved our differences in a meaningful way. A third party in the room would have helped us fight for a settlement rather than fight each other.

Instead, we continued down our war path, locked into our various positions, getting our families and friends to see our sides. Our divorce became the talk of the neighborhood—how embarrassing. In the end, it took more than a year to finalize our divorce but that wasn't the end of the story. Although I was satisfied with the results, my "spouse" was not. His needs hadn't been adequately addressed.

So a few years later, he filed motions for modifications to parenting time, followed by motions for modifications for child support. I just wanted him to "leave me alone" and he wanted justice. After another year or two of hiring CFI's (child and family investigators) and finding new attorneys to represent us, we received another set of court orders. This time, I felt my needs weren't met and I paid dearly (emotionally, physically and financially) for this unpleasant experience.

Hopefully, the wisdom in the pages of this book can prevent you from going down a long, tiresome, less-than-rewarding path towards divorce. Many couples find ways to divorce in a manner that meets their financial and parental needs, as well as the emotional need to preserve their dignity and well-being during what can be a grueling process. I hope this latter path can become the one that you follow.

NOBODY PLANS TO DIVORCE

Currently half of all marriages end in divorce. Yet we don't plan to divorce, so few of us have much information about the better and worse paths to traverse during a divorce. We essentially have to learn "on the fly" as we are going through the process. I certainly didn't decide to add divorce to my "bucket list" of things I wanted to accomplish in life. However, I did get to experience divorce (twice as a matter of fact), and as I put my own teachings into practice, I gained a new appreciation for what works in theory and what works in reality. In this section of the book, I will share with you what works and why it works, as well as what you can do to lessen the negative impact of divorce while simultaneously strengthening the positive.

There's so much talk about the negative aspects of divorce. I wish we heard more about the positive. If a family successfully manages a divorce, the children can walk away from the experience as stronger, more capable people. On the other hand, when a couple stays in a high-conflict marriage, the "ice wars" can be more damaging to their children than solving the problem via divorce. Not only does divorce reduce the conflict, it allows parents to reach their full potential as individuals because they cease putting so much time and energy into a marriage that isn't working. In turn, they are able to put more time and energy into their children.

YOUR SUPPORT SYSTEM

One of the most important things you can do is establish a support system for yourself. If there's a silver lining to the fact that half of marriages currently choose divorce, it's that there's more and more support for individuals going through this transition. If your venue is self-help books, there are plenty to choose from. One of my favorites is Bruce Fisher's *Rebuilding, When Your Relationship Ends.*

If you like therapy or coaching, plenty of counselors specialize in helping families get through the divorce process. Coaching people through the pathways of divorce has become a popular alternative to traditional counseling. It focuses more specifically on how to traverse the paths of divorce as opposed to gaining insight and in-depth understanding about what makes you tick. Having someone to talk to who can provide wisdom around both the emotional and physical aspects of divorce can be invaluable as you work towards rebuilding your life.

Friends and family can also offer a significant support system as can groups and classes which focus on surviving the divorce process. It is essential that you find a support system that works for you, not only for yourself but for your children. In essence, you will be their role model; you have the opportunity to demonstrate how to handle massive changes in life and cope with strong emotions. Plus if you are taking care of yourself, you will be better equipped to take care of your children and their needs.

KRISTINE TURNER

TELLING YOUR CHILDREN
ABOUT THE DIVORCE

Both parents need to tell their children about the divorce; re-telling the story is okay. Repeat the following message to them from time to time:

Divorce Is Final

It was an Adult Decision

It was Not Their Fault

Reassure them you are available and there for them. Children often wonder, "Can parents divorce me, too?" You need to make it clear to them that parents don't divorce their children. Provide an area or situation in which their voice is heard. This lets them know they matter. "Kids need their say, not necessarily their way."

LETTING YOUR CHILDREN
EXPRESS THEIR FEELINGS

Believe it or not, most parents only spend one and a half minutes per day actively listening to their children. Most of our time is spent giving instructions: "Set the table"; "Brush your teeth"; "Get into bed"; and so on. Try to become an active listener. Allow your children the time and freedom to express their feelings. Do not be afraid to ask about their negative feelings. Let them know that all their feelings are okay.

One of my favorite things I did with my children involved our bedtime routine. A couple of evenings a week, when I was putting them to bed, I would check in with them to see how they were coping with the divorce. I liked talking to them in the evenings because it was quiet and there weren't too many pressures on our time. Ask your children: "What was your high point today?" and "What was your low point today?" These kinds of questions can elicit conversation and often lead to helpful discussions.

Some families may prefer to have discussions around the dinner table, while others feel that car rides present good opportunities to discuss the divorce. Children often prefer the car because they don't have to look you in the eye; they are seated behind or next to you. Regardless of the method you choose, make sure that you build some time into your schedule to check in with you children on a regular basis.

And be careful not to make this time about you. Try not to "parentify" your children—don't make them your friend. They need to be your children and you need to be the parent. They need to know that they can depend on you for support, and that they don't need to take care of you. Your support should come from other adults and other sources.

TIP

NEVER try to get support from your children. They may try to be your friend out of their fear of abandonment, but in the end it will only confuse them. Children need to know that they can turn to you for support, not the other way around.

GIVING YOUR CHILDREN
ROUTINE AND CONSISTENCY

Provide your children with routine, consistency and dependability. As soon as you can, re-establish family rituals such as "Wednesday is pizza night." Play board or video games with them, watch their favorite TV shows together or read aloud from their favorite books. Routine gives children a sense of control and power in a healthy way.

This turned out to be my favorite part of the divorce. Once I got through the loss, I realized that I got to pick and choose all the activities at my house, with my children's input, of course. I found that I really didn't like some of the things we had been doing as a family such as fishing. I would leave that and camping and boating for their dad. We go to museums and travel to national parks (without the camping).

Another plus has been my parents' involvement. Now that I am single, they can come and go without causing any marital rift. My children get to see their grandparents on a regular basis, and I have a better bond my parents. In essence, we have two generations providing wisdom while raising the children.

Try to spend your time with the children instilling your values and priorities. You need to be dependable. Say what you mean and mean what you say (but don't say it mean). In short, do what you say you are going to do. You are your children's role model. The healthier emotionally you are, the more consistent you are at managing your new life, the better off your children will be as they work through this family transition.

FOOLS RUSH IN

Humans are social beings. There is a biological pull that many of us feel towards living with other people. It is tough to deny ourselves the bonds that cohabitation affords. We need others for support and nurturance. So it may not surprise you that around 85% of people go on to remarry within three to five years post their divorce.

What most of us do is remarry the same kind of person we just divorced. They have a different name and face, but the personality traits are similar. Something in your childhood or personality attracts you to certain types of people and you will usually continue that pattern unless you make a conscious attempt to alter it.

One way to do this is to develop your own "new IDENTITY." Allow yourself the gift of time, at least a couple of years to heal and rebuild your life. Learn about yourself before you start dating again; ask yourself tough questions: "Why was I attracted to my former spouse?"; "What worked in the marriage? Why?"; "What didn't work? Why?"; "What type of person am I better suited to be around?"; "What types of people are better for me to associate with? Why?"

By asking yourself these types of questions, you gain a better understanding about your relationship choices and why your choice in spouse ultimately didn't work out. You will also learn more about what you had hoped the marriage would fulfill for you. Can it be fulfilled without remarriage? Do you really want to remarry? Is dating without worrying about remarriage a better alternative for you?

As a psychologist who taught parenting after divorce classes, I thought I had it all figured out. When I went through my first divorce, I had been contemplating the problems for a couple of years. I thought I had done a lot of the healing work and thus made the mistake of quickly seeking comfort in a new relationship.

We have this natural tendency to want intimate connection, but we really need to give ourselves plenty of time to heal from one relationship before we get too serious about another. If I could do it all over again, I would date more people or simply go out with good friends and try new activities or hobbies. I would take the time to heal and learn from my past mistakes before rushing into a new marriage.

"The best advice I got during my divorce was to focus on the only thing that I could control, myself. It was hard to realize that I couldn't control my former spouse or my kids' reaction to the divorce. The only person I could control was me."

KEY POINTS TO REMEMBER

PARENTS CAN BE IN DIFFERENT EMOTIONAL STAGES OF DIVORCE:
(see page 15 for 5 Stages of Grief)

Going through these five emotional stages is a necessary process towards healing that may or may not go in the exact order listed above. So parents may not be in the same stage as each other. Children, however, always follow their parents through the stages; in other words, children cannot get to acceptance unless one of their parents does.

Sometimes one parent will get stuck in the anger stage. Anger is a secondary emotion that masks pain and sadness underneath. A person might be unwilling to experience sadness and fight to suppress it by staying angry, undermining any attempt to heal after a divorce. So it is vital that you make every attempt to heal yourself.

YOU SHOULD NEVER CRITICIZE THE OTHER PARENT:

Never criticize the other parent in front of your children. Because children see themselves as extensions of their parents, they often feel like you are criticizing them when you badmouth the other parent. I am often asked in my seminars how you can overcome a situation where the other parent is badmouthing you. Nobody wants to roll over and take it, especially from their "spouse."

The option I like best is to tell your children that you have a different viewpoint or opinion than the other parent. Make sure that you don't badmouth them in the process; simply say that you see things differently and that having different opinions is perfectly normal. Then your children are free to choose how to interpret the situation

Although children need to know that the divorce wasn't their fault, they don't need to know all the juicy details about why you chose to divorce. Don't tell children too many adult specifics about the divorce. It's better to say, "Mom and Dad aren't happy as husband and wife, and we want to put our energy into raising you instead of into the marriage. We think that this will help our family."

I realize that some of you feel like the divorce was not your choice. Divorce is usually easier when both parties want it, but on the flip side, you can't force someone to stay in a marriage when they want out. It won't lead to "happily ever after." In this case, you may struggle with what to say to your children. It's perfectly okay to say that you and your "spouse" wanted to solve the marital problems in different ways (you wanted counseling while he wanted a divorce); however, the end result is still divorce. The trick to saying this is to do it without badmouthing the other parent.

On a positive note, it is "music to their ears" when you say something nice about the other parent. Let your children know that you want them to love both parents and that you aren't going to get in the way of them having a loving relationship with Mom or Dad.

Another tact might be to say to your "spouse" (in the most loving way possible) something like, "I read a book that says it's not helpful to speak negatively about your former spouse in front of the children; I am going to practice this approach. Children need to love both of their parents and I intend to help foster that love."

LIMIT YOUR CHILDREN'S EXPOSURE TO CONFLICT:

Limit conflict at all costs. Familial conflict is one of the most damaging things we can do to our children. Nothing is worse for children than to witness their parents fighting in the driveway during a change in custody. If you think that you will fight, try to arrange for someone else to make the exchange or try using a neutral location as an alternative, such as school or daycare.

When you are dropping your children off with the other parent versus picking them up, take advantage of it. Send a subtle but important message by "giving" them to the other parent versus the other parent "taking" them away. Say something like, "Tell your dad 'hi' for me," or "Don't forget to give Dad the special treat we bought for him."

AVOID PARENTAL LOSS

The children who rarely see Mom or never see Dad after the divorce suffer tremendously. They grow up feeling incomplete, constantly wondering why their mom or dad doesn't want to spend time with them. It can lead to abandonment issues, relationship problems and low self-esteem well into their adult years, even causing them to pass on their difficulties to their children.

You may feel like using your "spouse's" behavior as a weapon to keep them from the children, even fight to deny them any parental rights. Unless the situation is extreme having to do with criminal activity or abusive actions, spare your children the loss of the other parent. But if the other parent has a drinking problem, for example, there are options to protect your children while allowing them to see Mom or Dad. Perhaps the court order can state your "spouse" cannot drive with the children in the car or cannot be with the children alone.

If you are in a situation where the other parent is absent by choice, all is not lost, but you will have to pick up some of the pieces. Let your children know that the divorce is not their fault and that their absent parent does love them: "Mom or Dad is not in a position to do much caretaking right now," or "Mom or Dad is working on healing before getting back into parenting again." By saying these things, you are helping your children see that they are still lovable, that the issues are not about them.

PARENTING PLANS

Developing a parenting plan is an essential part of the divorce process. It is important that children get plenty of access to each of their parents.

If both parents have been active and involved before the divorce, a more equal division of parenting time can occur. In situations where one parent has done the majority of the childcare, that parent should continue to be the primary parent until the children have time to adapt to spending more time with the secondary parent. Then, over time, it is feasible for the children to spend 50% of their time with each parent.

Keep in mind that the younger your children are, the harder it is for them to be away from a parent (particularly a primary parent) for long periods of time. Sometimes shorter, more frequent exchanges are helpful. As children get older, they can tolerate longer stays away from a parent. If siblings are going from Mom's house to Dad's house together, this makes the transitions easier for them. Younger children will often tolerate a more lengthy stay away from a parent if they have siblings with them. As children reach their "tween" and teen years, they are much more capable of a 50% parenting split.

Some parents prefer a week with the children and a week without. The positive aspect this plan offers is fewer transitions; families can settle into a routine for a longer period of time. The downside is the longer breaks children have from their parents. Consider that children's sense of time is quite different from an adult's. A week might rush by for you, but your child might think it's an eternity.

Another popular plan is a 5-2-2-5 plan where one parent has the kids on Monday and Tuesday, the other parent has the children on Wednesday and Thursday, and then Friday, Saturday and Sunday are alternated between Mom's house and Dad's house. This plan has consistency, but more transitions between households. It does, however, keep both parents involved in the children's lives on a weekly if not daily basis.

There are an infinite number of possible plans that might work for your family. Jobs, schools and other factors will have to be taken into account when developing your parenting plan.

Bottom line: Find a plan that works for the whole family—one in which your children can thrive.

Remember that you can still participate in your children's lives even when they aren't staying at your house. Go to their sporting events, practices, plays and rehearsals; volunteer at their school; call them on a regular basis; and send text messages or emails. Continue to build the relationship with them that you have always wanted.

> *"I try to say positive things about the kids' dad on occasion. It seems to be music to their ears, and it really reduces my negative feelings toward him."*

PARENTING CLASSES

PARENTING AFTER DIVORCE CLASSES:

In many states, courts mandate that divorcing parents attend a co-parenting after divorce class, often needing to see a certificate of completion. These classes are typically four hours long and focus on the best interest of the child.

Basically, these classes cover the positive and negative approaches to co-parenting after a divorce. They discourage things like badmouthing your "spouse" in front of the children and encourage being flexible and cooperative with each another.

(Online Class: www.NewBeginningsCoParenting.com)

HIGH-CONFLICT PARENTING CLASSES:

Many states also offer "level two" parenting classes for high-conflict cases. They can run from eight to twelve weeks, meeting weekly for an hour or two.

These classes tend to focus on co-parenting from a parallel approach, which is how to parent as individuals thereby minimizing the interaction between parents. These classes also point out the damage that can be done to children if the conflict between parents persists through the years.

USEFUL TIPS REITERATED

❖ Reassure your children that they will continue to have a relationship with both parents.
❖ Reassure your children that you will be available to them.
❖ Demonstrate your love on a daily basis.
❖ Show your children through your actions that you are trustworthy.
❖ Continue to set limits and discipline your children because structure is helpful to them.
❖ Listen to your children. Spend 20 minutes a day sitting quietly with your children, allowing them to talk about their day and their feelings. Make eye contact with them. Do not offer advice unless they ask for it.
❖ Encourage children to express their opinions.
❖ Encourage children to express their feelings (including sadness, loss, hurt, anger, guilt, helplessness or fear) even if what they say is hard to bear.
❖ Explain changes in concrete terms. Show them where each parent will live; reassure them that there will be enough food and money. Don't bother them with the details; refrain from sharing concerns about finances or residences with them.
❖ Keep children out of the middle.
❖ Help children adapt to both of their homes, for example, giving them a toothbrush, clothes, toys and books at both places.
❖ Communicate with the other parent about the children's issues.
❖ Develop a workable parenting plan that keeps both parents involved in their children's lives.

ABOUT THE DIVORCE TEAM

DAVID W. HECKENBACH, ESQ.
JAN PARSONS, MORTGAGE BANKER
KRISTINE TURNER, PH.D.
KURT GROESSER, REALTOR ®, MBA

DAVID W. HECKENBACH, ESQ.

Dave Heckenbach is a founding partner of Heckenbach Ammarell, LLP, which has been featured by *Forbes* magazine. His practice is primarily in the area of complicated divorce matters for individuals of high net worth and income. He has handled literally hundreds of contested hearings in cases involving divorce, paternity, allocation of parental responsibilities, post-decree modifications, child support modification, child support enforcement, maintenance modification, step-parent rights, and grandparent rights.

A trial lawyer for over 30 years specializing in complex litigation, Dave is best known as a formidable adversary in the courtroom, for his strategic abilities, and for the respect he commands from other attorneys and the judges. He has earned the title of "Super Lawyer" since that process began a number of years ago and has achieved that stature every consecutive year since. As such he is recognized by his peers as being in the top 5% of all attorneys in his community.

Dave is also known for his charity work, having been recognized as the top fundraiser for a Leukemia benefit and recipient of the Pacemaker award. He served on the board of the Alzheimer's Association, Cross and Clef ministries, and the American Heart Association of Colorado, for which he was board chairman and co-chairman for the Toyota celebrity ski challenge. He has also been listed in the Denver Social Register and Record since 1993.

Dave earned his Bachelor of Arts from Washington and Lee University in 1976, graduating cum laude with honors in Psychology (Psi Chi, the National Honors Society for Psychology). He received his Juris Doctorate from the University of Colorado School of Law in May, 1979.

KURT GROESSER,
REALTOR ®, MBA

Kurt Groesser has been involved in the real estate industry since 2003. He has experience in commercial real estate sales, property management, commercial leasing and residential real estate sales both as a principal and a broker.

In 2006, Kurt enhanced his skills when he graduated from Texas A&M University with an MBA. He holds a Bachelor's degree in marketing from the University of Colorado.

Kurt has been a licensed real estate broker in the State of Colorado since 2008. As an owner of commercial real estate and a broker, Kurt brings solid financial skills and practical experience to the real estate sales and investing process.

JAN PARSONS
SENIOR MORTGAGE BANKER

Jan Parsons has five years of mortgage loan experience specializing in assisting couples facing divorce. She has found that those who are going through divorce have particular needs and often a high degree of anxiety about keeping their current home or financing a new one. Having gone through a divorce herself, Jan understands how difficult it is to make educated decisions at such an emotional time.

As a Senior Mortgage Banker, Jan has the ability to lend in all 50 states. She has been an expert witness on a number of divorce cases and has amassed many hours of Continuing Legal Education in divorce law and the entire divorce process. Jan is a member of the Parker Chamber of Commerce and the Metro Denver Interdisciplinary Committee. In addition, she is a co-host of *New Beginnings, Life After Divorce*, a radio show for couples and families facing divorce (www.CastleRockRadio.com).

A longtime resident of Denver, Colorado, Jan is a single parent who enjoys spending time with her son, gardening, skiing, traveling, entertaining and volunteering for the Special Olympics.

KRISTINE TURNER, PH.D.

Kristine Turner graduated with a Ph.D. in clinical psychology from the Pacific Graduate School of Psychology, an APA accredited school affiliated with Stanford's program. She has worked since 1994 as a clinician in a wide variety of arenas including emergency services, group and individual therapy, leadership training, parental coaching, mediation and parenting after divorce classes for the courts. She has also appeared in court as an expert witness.

Kristine's primary passion is parenting after divorce—helping families traverse the rocky road of divorce, preparing countless parenting plans and performing personality evaluations and IQ tests for courts, mental health centers, schools and families going through divorce. As a divorced parent herself, her efforts have been focused on educating families about the better and worse paths to divorce.

Kristine practices in South Metro Denver, Colorado, and teaches weekly seminars, runs an on-line course for parents going through divorce, and appears regularly on TV Channel 2's *Everyday Show* and Douglas County's TV Channel 8. She also hosts her own radio show for families going through divorce, *New Beginnings, Life After Divorce* (www.CastleRockRadio.com). In addition, Kristine teaches high school leadership classes as well as leads anti-bullying summits in Douglas County.

Kristine is a member of the American Psychological Association, the Colorado Psychological Association and the Colorado Interdisciplinary Committee (formerly the MDICCC), an organization for mental health and legal professionals who deal with divorce-related issues. She also works with numerous county agencies and served as an elected official on her local school board for six years in Douglas County, Colorado.

Kristine has written two books on the subject of helping parents help their children cope with divorce: *Mommy and Daddy are Getting Divorced* (2010) and the *New Beginnings for Divorcing Parents Workbook*.

RESOURCES

The Divorce Team's Blog www.DivorceTeam.blogspot.com

David W. Heckenbach, Esq.
Heckenbach/Ammarell, LLP

7400 E. Orchard Rd., Ste 3025N
Greenwood Village, CO 80111
Phone: 303.858.8000
Fax: 303.858.8001
www.FamilyLawColorado.com

Kurt Groesser, Realtor ®, MBA

Phone: 303.481.4222
Kurtgroesser@KW.com
www.GranthamHomeTeam.com

Jan Parsons Senior Mortgage Banker

4600 S. Ulster, Ste. 300
Denver, CO 80237
Phone: 720.308.1320
Fax: 303.741.2150
JParsons@FirsTierBank.com
www.FirsTierBank.com

Kristine Turner, Ph.D.

558 Castle Pines Pkwy., Unit B4, #364
Castle Rock, CO 80108
Phone: 303.706.9424
Fax: 303.814.0365
Kristine.turner@NewBeginningsCoParenting.com
www.NewBeginningsCoParenting.com
www.DivorceAdviceforChildren.com   www.CastleRockRadio.com

Divorce Resolution Process

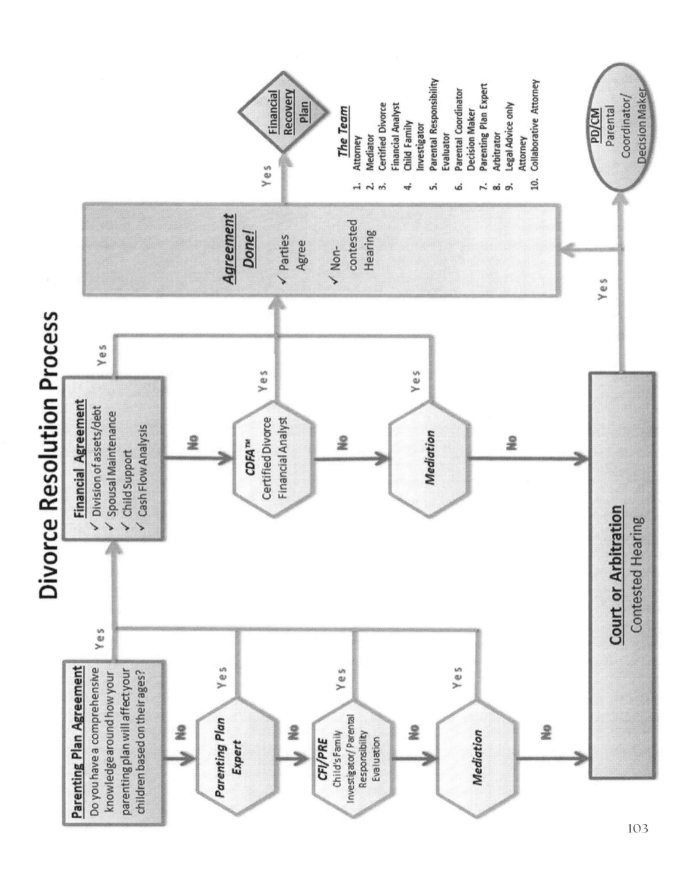

Financial Recovery Plan

The Team
1. Attorney
2. Mediator
3. Certified Divorce Financial Analyst
4. Child Family Investigator
5. Parental Responsibility Evaluator
6. Parental Coordinator Decision Maker
7. Parenting Plan Expert
8. Arbitrator
9. Legal Advice only Attorney
10. Collaborative Attorney

PD/CM
Parental Coordinator/ Decision Maker

Agreement Done!
✓ Parties Agree
✓ Non-contested Hearing

Financial Agreement
✓ Division of assets/debt
✓ Spousal Maintenance
✓ Child Support
✓ Cash Flow Analysis

CDFA™
Certified Divorce Financial Analyst

Mediation

Court or Arbitration
Contested Hearing

Parenting Plan Agreement
Do you have a comprehensive knowledge around how your parenting plan will affect your children based on their ages?

Parenting Plan Expert

CFI/PRE
Child's Family Investigator/ Parental Responsibility Evaluation

Mediation

Yes / No

Divorce Resolution Options	Pro Se	Mediation	Mediation with Financial & Legal Advice	Collaborative Divorce	Arbitration	Family Law Attorney	Court
Characteristics	• 'On Your Own' • Little to no outside professional advice	• Skilled neutral Mediator to facilitate discussion and agreement	• Skilled neutral professionals with resolution skills • Unbiased legal/financial services	• Both parties retain separate attorneys whose job it is to help them settle the dispute. No one may go to court.	• 3rd party makes decision with unresolved positions	• Attorney involved in entire process • Represents your best interest	• Judge will make decision on contested positions to reach settlement • Occurs when settlement cannot be reached
Advantages	• Low cost • You control family and financial decisions	• You have control of family and financial decisions • Mediator's goal is to reach agreement • Memorandums of understanding/ separation agreement generation • High resolution rate	• You control family and financial Decisions • Memorandum of understanding/ separation agreement generation • Financial Plan with future cash flow projections • Fixed fee for legal advice • Neutrality tends to facilitate a more equitable & amicable agreement	• If agreement is not reached, collaborative law process and attorneys terminate – incentive to resolve	• Settlement can be reached sooner than court system • In some cases, Arbitrator is a former judge • Negotiation skill	• Knowledge of legal process and divorce law • Negotiation skill • High accuracy on completion of required court documents	
Disadvantages	• Possible poor quality separation agreement including parenting/ financial plan • You generate and submit all court documents	• Agreement doesn't always mean best resolution • Limited financial and legal guidance	• No legal representation just legal advice • Neutrality tends to foster best interest outcomes rather than defending positions	• Can be time consuming and expensive • If settlement not reached, collaborative attorney is terminated and traditional divorce process begins	• Decision control is delegated to 3rd party • Outcome may not be in your or family's best interest • Arbitrator may not be an expert in financial/family matters	• Attorney will represent your best interest not necessarily the family • Not an expert in family and financial matters • Cost	• Decision control is delegated to judge – "you roll the dice" • Outcome may not be in your or families best interest • High cost
Conflict Level	Low	Low to Moderate	Low to Moderate	Low to Moderate	Moderate to High	High	Very High
Cost (estimate)	<$500	$800	$1,400 to $4,000	$15,000+	$5000+	$15,000+	$20,000+

Parenting Plan Dispute Resolution Tools	CFI *Child Family Investigator*	PRE *Parental Responsibility Evaluation*	PC/DM *Parenting Coordinator/ Decision Maker*
Characteristics	• Pre- decree (before finalization) family evaluation with parenting plan recommendation	• Pre- decree (before finalization) family evaluation with parenting plan recommendation • More in-depth and time consuming than a CFI evaluation	• Post decree (after divorce) • Skilled professional acts like a judge to decide any future disputes in the case
Cost (estimate)	$2000	$5000	$200/Hr.

Conscious Uncoupling

Dr. Habib Sadeghi & Dr. Sherry Sami

Divorce is a traumatic and difficult decision for all parties involved—and there's arguably no salve besides time to take that pain away. However, when the whole concept of marriage and divorce is reexamined, there's actually something far more powerful—and positive—at play.

The media likes to throw around the statistic that 50% of all marriages end in divorce. It turns out that's accurate: Many people are concerned about the divorce rate and see it as an important problem that needs to be fixed. But what if divorce itself isn't the problem? What if it's just a symptom of something deeper that needs our attention? The high divorce rate might actually be a calling to learn a new way of being in relationships.

UNTIL DEATH DO US PART

During the upper Paleolithic period of human history (roughly 50,000BC to 10,000BC) the average human life expectancy at birth was 33.[i] By 1900, U.S. life expectancy was only 46 for men, and 48 for women. Today, it's 76 and 81 respectively.[ii] During the 52,000 years between our Paleolithic ancestors and the dawn of the 20th Century, life expectancy rose just 15 years. In the last 114 years, it's increased by 43 years for men, and 48 years for women.

What does this have to do with divorce rates? For the vast majority of history, humans lived relatively short lives—and accordingly, they weren't in relationships with the same person for 25 to 50 years. Modern society adheres to the concept that marriage should be lifelong; but when we're living three lifetimes compared to early humans, perhaps we need to redefine the construct. Social research suggests that because we're living so long, most people will have two or three significant long-term relationships in their lifetime.

To put in plainly, as divorce rates indicate, human beings haven't been able to fully adapt to our skyrocketing life expectancy. Our biology and psychology aren't set up to be with one person for four, five, or six decades. This is not to suggest that there aren't couples who happily make these milestones—we all hope that we're one of them. Everyone enters into a marriage with the good intention to go all the way, but this sort of longevity is the exception, rather than the rule. Accomplishing that requires occasionally redefining who we are separately within the relationship and discovering new ways of being together as we change and grow. It's important to remember too, that just because someone is still married doesn't mean they're happy or that the relationship is fulfilling. To that end, living happily ever after for the length of a 21st century lifetime should not be the yardstick by which we define a successful intimate relationship: This is an important consideration as we reform the concept of divorce.

END OF THE HONEYMOON

Nearly everyone comes into a new marriage idealizing their partner. Everything is perfect in their minds because they've misidentified what marriage is really about. As far as they're concerned, they've found the love of their life, the person who understands them completely. Yes, there will be hiccups in the process, but by and large, there's no more learning left to do. They'll both be the same people 10 or 20 years from now as they are today. When we idealize our partners, things initially go very well as we subconsciously project our own positive qualities, as well as the qualities we wish we had, onto them. This positive projection, as it's called, happens during the honeymoon phase of the relationship where both partners can do no wrong in each other's eyes.

Sooner or later, the honeymoon ends and reality sets in, so does negative projection. This is usually when we stop projecting positive things onto our partners and begin to project our negative issue onto them instead. Unfortunately, this creates a boomerang effect as these negative issues always come right back to us, triggering our unconscious and long-buried negative internal objects, which are our deepest hurts, betrayals, and traumas. This back-and-forth process of projection and aggravation can escalate to the point where it impacts our psychic structure with even more trauma.

For most of us, these old unresolved issues can be traced back to our first intensely emotional relationship, the one we had with our parents. Because most of these old wounds are unconscious to us as adults, we're subconsciously driven to resolve them, which is why many people end up with partners that are very similar in key ways to their mother or father. If we're not in tune with this type of dynamic within our relationship, all we end up seeing is the repeated mistrust, abandonment, or other issue that's followed us through all our previous relationships. We never see that it's the signal to heal the emotional wound that's connected to it. Instead, we choose to blame the other person.

Because we believed so strongly in the "until death do us part" concept, we see the demise of our marriage as a failure, bringing with it shame, guilt, or regret. Since most of us don't want to face what we see as a personal failure, we retreat into resentment and anger, and resort to attacking each other instead. We've put on our armor and we're ready to do battle. What we don't realize is that while a full body shield may offer a level of self-protection, it's also a form of self-imprisonment that locks us inside a life that repeats the same mistakes over and over again. This includes attracting the same kind of partners to push the same emotional buttons for us until we recognize the deeper purpose of such a relationship.

INTIMACY & INSECTS

To understand what life is really like living with an external shield, we have to examine the experts: Insects. Beetles, grasshoppers, and all other insects have an exoskeleton. The structure that protects and supports their body is on the outside. Not only are they stuck in a rigid, unchanging form that provides no flexibility, they are also at the mercy of their environment. If they find themselves under the heel of a shoe, it's all over. That's not the only downside: Exoskeletons can calcify, leading to buildup and more rigidity.

By contrast, vertebrates like dogs, horses, and humans have an endoskeleton. Our support structure is on the inside of our bodies, giving us exceptional flexibility and mobility to adapt and change under a wide range of circumstances. The price for this gift is vulnerability: Our soft outside is completely exposed to hurt and harm every day.

Life is a spiritual exercise in evolving from an exoskeleton for support and survival to an endoskeleton. Think about it. When we get our emotional support and wellbeing from outside ourselves, everything someone says or does can set us off and ruin our day. Since we can't control or predict what another person does, our moods are at the mercy of our environment. We can't adapt to the situation if our intimate partner doesn't behave the way we think they should. Everything is then perceived as a personal attack and attempt to upset us. Up goes our armor and it's all-out war. When we feel unloved and unsupported, our antagonism is in full swing and needs a target. Either rightly or wrongly, that usually ends up being the person closest to us, our intimate partner.

With an internal support structure, we can stand strong because our stability doesn't depend on anything outside ourselves. We can be vulnerable and pay attention to what's happening around us, knowing that whatever comes, we have the flexibility to adapt to the situation. There's a reason we call cowards spineless: It takes great courage to drop your armor, expose your soft inside, and come to terms with the reality of what's happening around you. It's a powerful thing to then realize that you can survive it. When we examine our intimate relationships from this perspective, we realize that they aren't for finding static, lifelong bliss like we see in the movies. They're for helping us evolve a psycho-spiritual spine, a divine endoskeleton made from conscious self-awareness so that we can evolve into a better life without recreating the same problems for ourselves again and again. When we learn to find our emotional and spiritual support from inside ourselves, nothing that changes our environment or relationships can unsettle us. Situations we once viewed as problems will be seen as opportunities to reflect inwardly and determine what each circumstance is trying to reveal to us about ourselves. Problems are transmuted into opportunities for growth.

There's a scientific theory by Russian esotericist, Peter Ouspensky, that the creation of insects was a failed attempt by nature to evolve a higher form of consciousness. There was a time millions of years ago when insects were enormous—a dragonfly's wings were three feet across. So why didn't they end up being the dominant species on earth? Because they lacked flexibility, which is what evolution is all about, and couldn't adapt to changing conditions like humans can. The lives of people who imprison themselves in an exoskeleton of anger usually don't evolve the way they'd like them to, either. Being trapped inside negative energy like anger and resentment keeps people from moving forward in life because they can only focus on the past. Even worse, over time, these powerful emotions often turn into disease in the body.

CONSCIOUS UNCOUPLING

To change the concept of divorce, we need to release the belief structures we have around marriage that create rigidity in our thought process. The belief structure is the all-or-nothing idea that when we marry, it's for life. The truth is, the only thing any of us have is today. Beyond that, there are no guarantees. The idea of being married to one person for life, especially without some level of awareness of our unresolved emotional needs, is too much pressure for anyone. In fact, it would be interesting to see how much easier couples might commit to each other by thinking of their relationship in terms of daily renewal instead of a lifetime investment. This is probably the reason why so many people say their long-term relationships changed overnight, once they got married. The people didn't change, but the expectation did. It's odd that most of us assume that everything in a relationship will stay the same based on a single promise made during a wedding ceremony and that somehow, no further work is required for the marriage to remain intact.

If we can recognize that our partners in our intimate relationships are our teachers, helping us evolve our internal, spiritual support structure, we can avoid the drama of divorce and experience what we call a conscious uncoupling. The idea of uncoupling as an alternative to a nasty divorce has been around since the 1970's. In 1990, author Diane Vaughan further defined the concept while psychotherapist, Katherine Woodward Thomas would popularize it a few years later. In these previous theories, uncoupling is rooted in how to part amicably, keeping mutual respect as part of the process and remembering the needs of any children involved. While these are admirable and necessary steps for a conscious uncoupling, to us, self-reflection must be the foundation of the process if we are to avoid repeating the same problems in the next relationship. The idea of conscious uncoupling is to gain enough self-awareness that we no longer have to do it anymore because we've now found ourselves in a fulfilling, sustainable, long-term relationship.

For our purposes, conscious uncoupling is the ability to understand that every irritation and argument within a relationship was a signal to look inside ourselves and identify a negative internal object that needed healing. Because present events always trigger pain from a past event, it's never the current situation that needs the real fixing. It's just the echo of an older emotional injury. If we can remain conscious of this during our uncoupling, we will understand it's how we relate to ourselves internally as we go through an experience that's the real issue, not what's actually happening.

From this perspective, there are no bad guys, just two people, each playing teacher and student respectively. When we understand that both are actually partners in each other's spiritual progress, animosity dissolves much quicker and a new paradigm for conscious uncoupling emerges, replacing the traditional, contentious divorce. It's only under these circumstances that loving co-parenting can happen. It's conscious uncoupling that prevents families from being broken by divorce and creates expanded families that continue to function in a healthy way outside of traditional marriage. Children are imitators by nature, and we teach what we are. If we are to raise a more conscious and civilized generation, we must model those behaviors through the choices we make during the good and bad times in our relationships.

WHOLENESS IN SEPARATION

It seems ironic to say that a marriage coming apart is the cause of something else coming together, but it's true. Conscious uncoupling brings wholeness to the spirits of both people who choose to recognize each other as their teacher. If they do, the gift they receive from their time together will neutralize their negative internal object that was the real cause of their pain in the relationship. Actually, this dynamic is in play in all of our personal relationships, not just the intimate ones. If we can allow ourselves this gift, our exoskeleton of protection and imprisonment will fall away and offer us the opportunity to begin constructing an endoskeleton, an internal cathedral, with spiritual trace minerals like self-love, self-acceptance, and self-forgiveness. This process allows us to begin projecting something different into the world because we've regained a missing part of our heart. This addition to our psychic infrastructure creates a wholeness that supports our own growth and ability to co-parent consciously.

COMING TOGETHER

The misunderstandings involved in divorce also have much to do with the lack of intercourse between our own internal masculine and feminine energies. Choosing to hide within an endoskeleton and remain in attack mode requires a great imbalance of masculine energy. Feminine energy is the source of peacemaking, nurturing, and healing. Cultivating your feminine energy during this time, regardless of whether you're a man or a woman, is beneficial to the success of conscious uncoupling. When our masculine and feminine energies reach equilibrium once more, we can emerge from our old relationship and consciously call in someone who reflects our new world, not the old one.

Naturally, divorce is much easier if both parties choose to have a conscious uncoupling. However, your experience and personal growth isn't conditional on whether or not your spouse chooses to participate. You can still receive the lessons he or she has to give you, resist being baited into dramatic arguments, and stand firm in your internal, spiritual support system. By choosing to handle your uncoupling in a conscious way, regardless of what's happening with your spouse, you'll see that although it looks like everything is coming apart; it's actually all coming back together.

[i] Hillard Kaplan, Kim Hill, Jane Lancaster, and A. Magdalena Hurtado (2000). A Theory of Human Life History Evolution: Diet, Intelligence and Longevity". Evolutionary Anthropology 9 (4): 156–185. doi:10.1002/1520-6505(2000)9:43.0.CO;2-7.

[ii] Centers for Disease Control and Prevention (2011). Life expectancy at birth, at age 65, and at age 75, by sex, race, and Hispanic origin: United States, selected years 1900-2010. National vital statistics system . United states 2011 web updates Washington D.C.: National center for healthcare statistics. http://www.cdc.gov/nchs/data/hus/2011/022.pdf.

Thank you for taking the time to learn about how to have a Smart Divorce.

If you found this to be a helpful resource: Please leave a review on Amazon.com

35827736R00064

Made in the USA
San Bernardino, CA
06 July 2016